Lilies

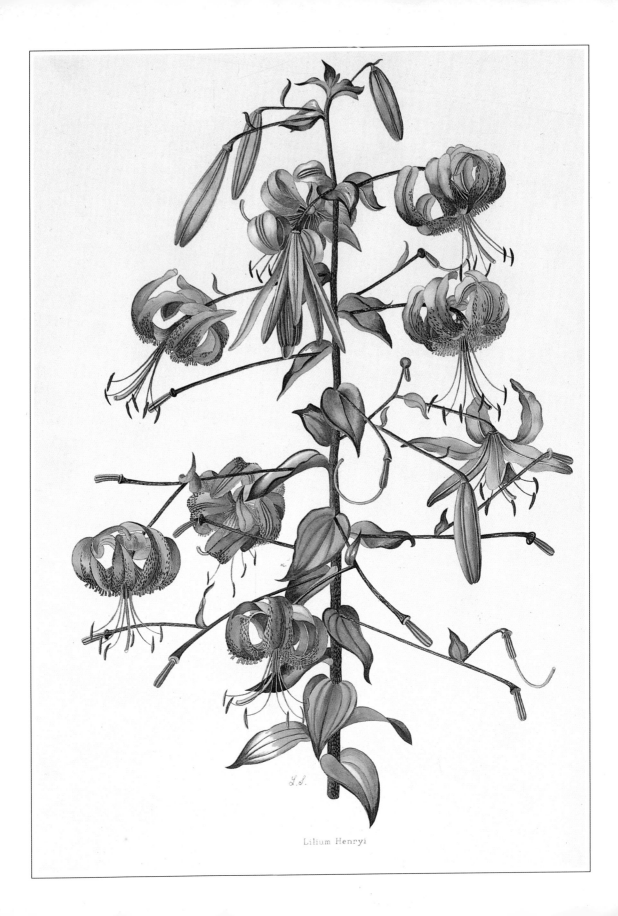

Lilium Henryi

KEW GARDENING GUIDES

Lilies

Victoria Matthews

Series editor John Simmons
OBE, VMH

The Royal Botanic Gardens, Kew
in association with
COLLINGRIDGE

Front cover photograph by Andrew Lawson (Golden Splendor Strain)
Back cover photograph by Victoria Matthews ('Lake Tulare')

Published in 1989 by Collingridge Books,
an imprint of The Hamlyn Publishing Group Limited,
Michelin House, 81 Fulham Road, London SW3 6RB, England
in association with the Royal Botanic Gardens, Kew.

ISBN 0 600 55766 9

Filmset in England by Servis Filmsetting Limited
in 11 on 12 pt Bembo

Printed in Hong Kong by Mandarin Offset

Contents

Lilium japonicum

Foreword

Gardening is in part instinctive, in part experience. Look in any village or town and you will see many gardens, balconies or even windowsills full of healthy plants brightening up the streets. However, there are always likely to be other plots that are sterile and devoid of plants, or overgrown and unloved. Admittedly gardening is laborious, but the hours spent sweating behind a mower on a hot summer's day will be amply rewarded when the smooth green lawn is admired; the painful nettle stings incurred while clearing ground will soon be forgotten when the buds of newly planted shrubs burst forth in spring.

These few examples of the joy and pain of gardening are all part of its attraction to its devotees. The successful gardeners and plant lovers of this world come to understand plants instinctively, learning their likes and dislikes, their lifespan and ultimate size, recognizing and correcting ailments before they become serious. They work with the seasons of the year, not against them; they think ahead, driven by caring, being aware of when conditions are right for planting, mowing or harvesting and, perhaps most important of all, they know when to leave well alone.

This understanding of the natural order cannot be learned overnight. It is a continuous two-way process that lasts a lifetime. In creating a garden, past masters such as Humphry Repton in the eighteenth century or Gertrude Jekyll in the nineteenth perceived and enhanced the natural advantages of a site, and Jekyll in particular was an acute observer of the countryside and its seasons. Seeing a plant in its natural situation gives knowledge of its needs in cultivation. And then, once design and planting have formed a garden, the process reverses as the garden becomes the inspiration for learning about the natural world.

With the widespread loss of the world's natural habitats now causing the daily extinction of species, botanic gardens and other specialist gardens are becoming as arks, holding irreplaceable collections. Thus gardens are increasingly cooperating to form networks which can retain as great a diversity of plants as possible. More than ever gardens can offer a refuge for our beleaguered flora and fauna and, whether a garden be great or small, formal or natural, this need should underpin its enduring qualities of peace and harmony – the challenge of the creative unison of formal and natural areas.

The authors of these volumes have all become acknowledged specialists in particular aspects of gardening or botany, and their texts draw on their experience and impart the vitality that sustains their own enthusiasm and dedication. Throughout its long history of achievement in botanical science Kew has also concerned itself with education through its renowned School of Horticulture and the broader dissemination of plants and plant-related information. It is hoped, therefore, that these *Kew Gardening Guides* will be a further means of sharing the hard-earned knowledge and understanding of specialists with a wider audience.

John Simmons
Editor

Opposite: *Lilium japonicum* by Lilian Snelling from the *Supplement* to Elwes' *Monograph of the Genus Lilium*. This is one of the few species with clear pink flowers and, as its name implies, comes from Japan (see also page 81)

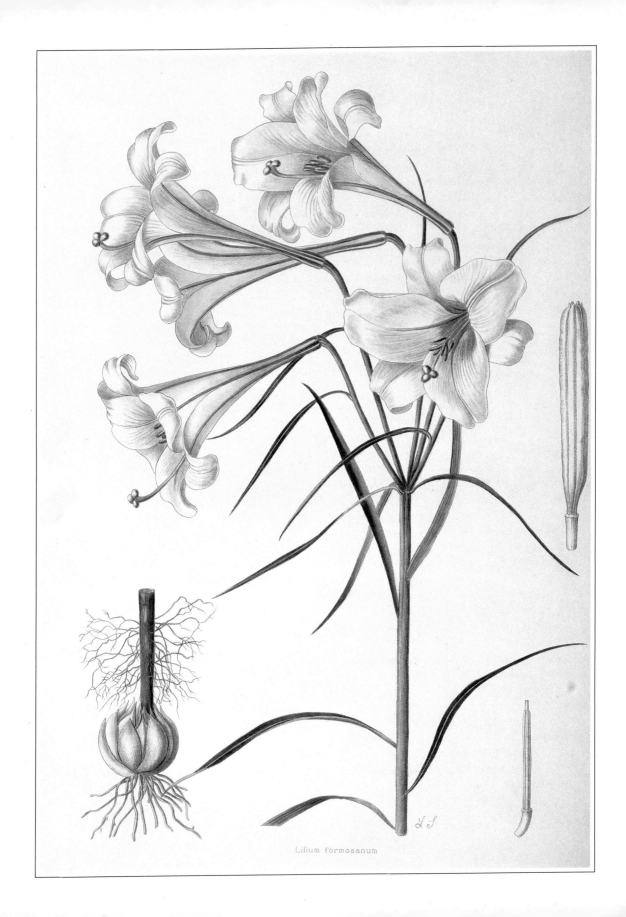

Lilium formosanum

Introduction

Lilies are among the most beautiful of flowering plants and are deservedly popular, adding interest and elegance to the garden.

The genus *Lilium*, which is widespread throughout the temperate zone of the northern hemisphere, includes plants whose flowers vary considerably in shape – they can be bowl-shaped, star-shaped, trumpet-shaped or in the form of a 'turk's-cap'. This variation in flower type, combined with the wide range of colours available, gives the gardener an enormous choice when he selects lilies for the garden. In the wild lilies grow in a variety of habitats, and knowledge of the habitat acts as a pointer to the way in which the plants should be cultivated.

One of the bonus features of lilies is that their flowers are relatively long-lasting. A plant can produce flowers over several weeks, and the flowers are generally tough and weather-resistant. The long-lasting characteristic makes lilies invaluable as cut flowers – they are often used in church decoration, where the arrangements can remain for some time. They are also popular for bouquets as, unlike many flowers, they last well out of water and do not droop.

For years lilies have suffered from the reputation of being difficult plants to grow, and many gardeners have been discouraged by stories of pests and diseases launching fatal attacks from all sides. Certainly, many lilies *are* prone to such attacks, but modern pesticides and fungicides are extremely effective. There are also some species and hybrids that are disease-resistant and need minimal attention, flowering reliably year after year. There is therefore no reason why even the smallest garden should not boast at least a few of these attractive plants. The beginner should start with easy lilies, which include *L. martagon*, *L. regale*, 'Enchantment' or the Mid-Century Hybrids. After success with these, more demanding lilies can be tried.

This book is written mainly for gardeners who wish to grow lilies out of doors, though details of greenhouse cultivation are also provided. The impressive giant Himalayan lilies, which belong to the genus *Cardiocrinum*, have been included because they are so closely related to lilies; indeed, in the past they were regarded as belonging to the genus *Lilium*.

The last 50 years have seen a boom in the production of lily cultivars, and lily-breeders in many countries are continuing to produce new plants whose flowers have even better colour, shape or perfume. They are also aiming at improvement in such desirable features as sturdiness or resistance to disease. More cultivars are now available than ever before, and these are helping to relieve some of the pressure on the species, some of which are threatened in their wild habitats. The future of the lily is bright. Lily bulbs are now easily obtainable, available not only from specialist growers and bulb dealers but also from garden centres and even chain stores. The latter sources are fine, provided that the bulbs are carefully examined before being purchased.

If you have never grown lilies before, then beware! An increasing body of evidence suggests that lily-growing results in an addiction that is very hard to break. The addict also develops a compulsion to influence and convert others. The author cannot be held responsible for the consequences of introducing these extraordinarily beautiful and exciting plants into your garden.

Opposite: *Lilium formosanum* by Lilian Snelling from the *Supplement* to Elwes' *Monograph of the Genus Lilium*. It has the great advantage of producing flowers in the first year after seed sowing (see also page 80)

1
The Lily in History

The history of the lily goes back a long way. Frescoes (dating from 1550 to 1450 BC) with representations of lilies were found at the Palace of Minos at Knossos and at nearby Amnisos in Crete, as were vases decorated with lilies. It is likely that the lily which inspired this ornamentation was the Madonna lily, *L. candidum*. The same lily was mentioned in the work of ancient Greek and Roman writers. Pliny wrote about it, and was the first to describe how the white flowers could be changed to purple by soaking the bulbs in red wine. *L. candidum* was grown not only for its beautiful and fragrant flowers but also for medicinal purposes, such as reducing inflammation and softening corns.

It is generally accepted that the Romans brought *L. candidum* to Britain. It was known to the monks of medieval times and has been associated with several saints; because in Christian symbolism it represented purity, chastity and innocence, it eventually became the special flower of the Virgin. Its resultant common name, the Madonna lily, is more recent, of 19th century origin. *L. candidum* was frequently included in paintings of the Annunciation, from the Middle Ages to Victorian times.

Opposite: *Lilium candidum*, the Madonna lily, which has probably been in cultivation longer than any other species (see also page 77)

Left: *Lilium pyrenaicum*, here growing wild in south-western France. It flowers early in the lily season (see also page 89)

Chaucer, and later Shakespeare, knew only *L. candidum*. By 1596, however, John Gerard, author of the famous *Herball*, was familiar with *L. bulbiferum*, *L. chalcedonicum* and *L. martagon*, all European species. Some thirty years later two more species from Europe, *L. pomponium* and *L. pyrenaicum*, had been introduced into English gardens, as well as *L. canadense* from North America, which is thought to have been introduced into Europe by the French. The bright orange colour and mid summer flowering of *L. bulbiferum*, the orange lily, caused it to be associated with the Ulster Orangemen, who every July celebrate the victory of William of Orange over the Irish Catholics in 1691.

ASIAN LILIES

The first Asian lily to appear in cultivation was *L. dauricum*, some time around 1740. The tiger lily, *L. lancifolium*, was sent back from Canton in 1804 by William Kerr, who went to the Far East in 1803 to collect plants for Kew Gardens. Sir Joseph Banks, who was then the unofficial scientific director of the Royal Botanic Gardens, Kew, recognizing its horticultural value, arranged for the propagation and distribution of over ten thousand bulbs.

In 1862 the nurseryman John Gould Veitch introduced *L. auratum*, the golden-rayed lily of Japan, and astounded the European gardening world, which had never before seen anything like it. Immediately there was a huge demand for the bulbs; the Japanese responded by raising large numbers, which were overfed and grown 'soft'. *L. auratum* is naturally rather prone to virus diseases, and these weaker bulbs quickly succumbed, giving the species a reputation for being difficult to cultivate. This reputation unfortunately spread to the whole genus, and lilies fell out of favour for about forty years – until *L. regale* restored lilies to their rightful place.

In 1903 *L. regale* was introduced by Ernest Henry Wilson (1876–1930), who was given the nickname 'Chinese' Wilson because of his successful explorations for plants in that country. The story of the discovery of this lily demonstrates some of the hardships that plant-hunters have had to endure in the search for beautiful plants to adorn our gardens. Wilson found the lily in the inaccessible Min valley in western China, where it grew in tens of thousands. Having dug up some bulbs, he was caught by a landslide and his leg was broken in two places. He lay injured on a narrow mountain path, unable to move as a 40-strong mule train approached and then stepped over him. To his enormous relief, the mules avoided trampling on him. Eventually, camera tripod legs were used as splints and Wilson's porters carried him to a medical missionary. The leg healed slowly and badly, and almost had to be amputated. Luckily, both the leg and the lilies survived this experience! Wilson, however, retained what he referred to as his 'lily limp' for the rest of his life.

TWENTIETH-CENTURY INTRODUCTIONS

The first half of the 20th century saw an explosion in plant-collecting, especially in China. The names Wilson, Forrest, Farrer, Henry, Kingdon Ward, Rock and Ludlow and Sherriff are famous in the annals of plant exploration and introduction. During this time many beautiful lilies were sent back to Britain:

'Chinese' Wilson introduced *L. duchartrei*, *L. davidii* and *L. sargentiae*; George Forrest (1873–1932) brought back *L. taliense* and *L. henrici*; Reginald Farrer (1880–1920) was responsible for *L. leucanthum* var. *centifolium*; Augustine Henry (1857–1930) introduced *L. henryi* and *L. leucanthum*; Frank Kingdon Ward (1885–1958) found *L. mackliniae* and *L. wardii*; Joseph Rock (1884–1962) found the extraordinarily dark-flowered *L. papilliferum*; the joint explorations of Frank Ludlow (1885–1972) and George Sherriff (1898–1967) yielded *L. sherriffiae*, named after Sherriff's wife, Betty. Some species proved to be extremely difficult to grow, and died out in gardens after only a few years.

In recent years, plantsmen have been permitted to enter China once again. In 1986 a joint expedition between the Botanic Gardens of Kew and Edinburgh and the Kunming Institute of Botany in China resulted in the reintroduction into cultivation of *L. soulei* and *L. lophophorum*, unusual species that had not survived their earlier introduction. It is to be hoped that improved horticultural techniques and particular care will result in the return of these lilies to a permanent place in our gardens.

ILLUSTRATION

Lily-fanciers are lucky in that one of the most beautiful and impressive monographs ever written features the lily, and contains some of the finest illustrations produced during the 19th century. The author was Henry John Elwes (1846–1922), a Gloucestershire landowner, traveller and collector whose passion for game-shooting eventually gave way to plant-hunting and gardening. He had a particular interest in bulbs, and species of *Galanthus*, *Fritillaria* and *Hippeastrum* were named after him.

Elwes' *Monograph of the genus Lilium* was published in two volumes in 1877–1880. It is large, measuring 54.5×37.5 cm ($21\frac{1}{2} \times 14\frac{3}{4}$ in), and Elwes was most fortunate in acquiring the services of Walter Hood Fitch as illustrator. Fitch was an extremely prolific botanical artist who executed over 3000 lithographs for *Curtis's Botanical Magazine*. His illustrations for Elwes' book are some of the best he produced and demonstrate the enormous vitality with which his work is imbued, although not at the expense of scientific accuracy. These lithographs were beautifully coloured by hand.

After the death of Elwes, when new lilies had been introduced from the wild, supplements to the *Monograph* were published between 1933 and 1962. The earlier ones (still with hand-coloured lithographs) were illustrated by Lilian Snelling, three of which are reproduced in this book on the frontispiece and on pages 10 and 12, and the later ones (using modern colour printing) by Margaret Stones.

Unfortunately for those who do not possess it, this desirable *Monograph* is expensive. At an auction in London in 1987, a copy was sold for £8800 – more than twice the estimated price!

Pub. by W. Curtis, St. Geo. Crescent Apr. 1. 1794.

2
Lilies True and False

True lilies (which belong to the genus *Lilium* in the family Liliaceae) have a number of distinguishing characteristics. The bulb is made up of overlapping scales and lacks the bulb-tunic or coat possessed by most bulbs. The stem is unbranched and leafy, with the leaves scattered up the stem or arranged in whorls. The flower is composed of six perianth segments, which are free from one another at the base, where each has a nectar-bearing furrow or gland. There are six stamens, with versatile, dorsifixed anthers, i.e. the filament or stalk is attached to the back of the anther, more or less at its mid-point, so that the anther can move backwards and forwards. A single style connects the three-lobed stigma to the ovary. The fruit is a capsule containing numerous flat seeds.

ROOTS

Lilies produce roots of various kinds. The bulb has a basal plate, from the lower surface of which the feeder roots grow. These feeder roots are slender and usually much branched, and are the main means by which the plant obtains water and food. They usually occur around the edge of the basal plate, as do the contractile

Opposite: *Lilium catesbaei*, plate 259 from the *Botanical Magazine*. This beautiful and unusual lily comes from the south-eastern USA and is one of the more tender species, requiring winter protection in all but the warmest areas (see also page 77)

Left: Some lilies produce stem roots at the stem base, just above the bulb. Bulbs which are planted too shallowly may produce stem roots above soil level; if this happens compost should be heaped around the stem roots. The main functions of the contractile roots are to anchor the bulb securely in the soil and to pull it downwards into the ground. A seedling will begin its growth at or near the soil surface, and it is important that the bulb should eventually attain a suitable depth lower down. Contractile roots are larger and fatter than the feeder roots and usually have a corrugated or wrinkled surface. The contractile roots of a flowering-size bulb are important in preventing the bulb from moving upwards when the basal scales and the bottom of the basal plate die and disintegrate. They may eventually branch and change their function to feeder roots.

The third kind of roots found in lilies are the stem roots (see under stem).

BULBS

Lily bulbs differ from many more familiar bulbs in being made up of many fleshy scales, and not covered by a papery or leathery bulb-tunic such as that found in tulips or hyacinths. The lily bulb has a basal plate, from the lower surface of which roots are produced. The bulb-scales are attached to the upper surface. There is great variation in the shape and size of the scales, and in the degree to which they overlap. Some species have jointed scales. The scales are usually whitish, but in a few species they are yellow. Some bulbs become reddish purple if exposed to light.

There are several types of lily bulb.

Some lily bulbs are composed of jointed scales which usually have one or two joints

Concentric bulbs
The scales of the bulbs are arranged in a concentric pattern, and the growing point from which the stem arises is in the centre, as in *L. regale* and *L. martagon*.

Rhizomatous bulbs
These usually increase by branching, and the scales are arranged along the branches. Those that do not branch often 'grow' by forming two growing points. Really vigorous species can produce dense mats of bulbs. *L. pardalinum* is an example of a lily with a rhizomatous bulb.

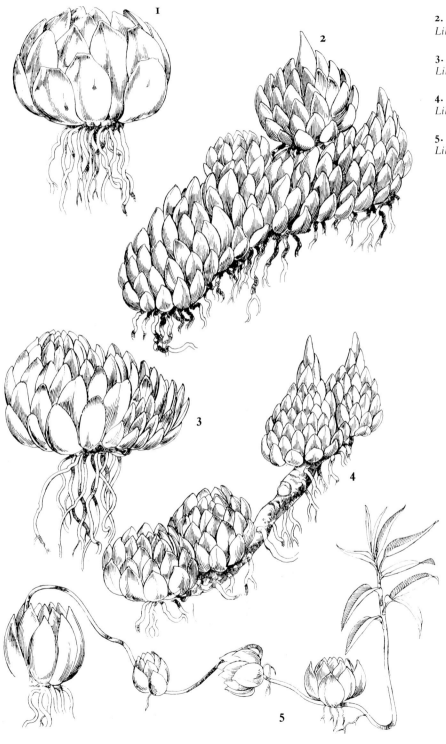

1. Concentric –
Lilium candidum

2. Rhizomatous –
Lilium pardalinum

3. Sub-rhizomatous –
Lilium humboldtii

4. Stoloniferous –
Lilium superbum

5. Stoloniform –
Lilium wardii

Sub-rhizomatous bulbs

These bulbs are intermediate between the concentric and rhizomatous types: the bulb expands in one direction rather than equally all round, e.g. *L. humboldtii*, *L. columbianum*.

Stoloniferous bulbs

Similar to the concentric type except that they produce a usually horizontal stolon below ground, at the end of which a new bulb is formed, e.g. *L. canadense*, *L. philadelphicum*.

Lilium duchartrei, a Chinese species with fragrant flowers, which grows most happily in areas with higher rainfall (see also page 79)

Lilium canadense, here growing among rhododendrons where its flowers help to cheer up the sombre foliage (see also page 76)

Stoloniform bulbs

These have stolons that grow through the soil horizontally and form concentric bulbs at intervals along their length, so a colony is soon built up. *L. duchartrei* and *L. wardii* are examples of this type.

BULBLETS AND BULBILS

In many species, bulblets are produced on the underground part of the stem, above the bulb. These can be detached and used for propagation. Bulbils (the name given to tiny bulbs produced on the part of the plant above the ground) are formed in the axils of the stem leaves of some species; often they produce small roots while still attached to the parent plant. In the autumn, as the stem withers, the bulbils fall to the ground, where they take root.

STEMS

Lily stems are always unbranched for most of their length, branching only at the top, where the flowers are produced. In many lilies, roots are produced just above the bulb on the bottom part of the stem, which tends to be thicker and rather tough in this area. The stem roots are small and thin in comparison with the feeder roots, and are much-branched. They help to anchor the plant and also play a part in nutrition. Stem-rooting lilies that have been planted too shallowly benefit from a mulch of leafmould mixed with compost, enabling the stem roots to function as feeders. When the stem dies at the end of the year, the stem roots die with it.

The leaves of lilies basically are arranged in two ways:
Left: whorled
Right: scattered

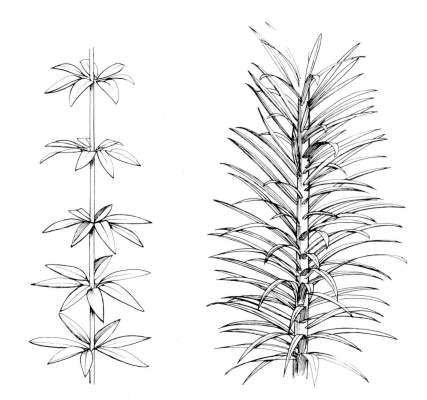

LEAVES

The leaves of lilies are usually stalkless, though there are exceptions (e.g. *L. speciosum* and *L. auratum*), and vary from very narrow to broadly oval. They have parallel veins, which run from the base to the apex and in some species are hairy or papillate on the underside of the leaf. Hairs or papillae are occasionally present on the margin, for example in *L. pomponium*. Lily leaves have between one and nine veins; each species and hybrid has its own typical number.

There are two main ways in which the leaves are arranged (see above) – scattered, in which the leaves are evenly distributed around and up the stem, and whorled, in which they are borne like wheel-spokes at intervals up the stem, with bare stem between. Some lilies have a mixture of whorled and scattered leaves.

FLOWERS

All lilies have flowers with parts in threes. What appear to be six petals are in fact three sepals on the outside of the flower (they enclose the petals in the bud), and three petals which are usually a little broader. Together they make up the perianth of the flower, and are known as perianth segments. Each segment has a groove at the base where nectar is produced. In some lilies this 'nectary furrow' is bordered by papillae or hairs. The tips of the segments are usually papillate or occasionally hairy. The segments of most lilies are narrowly oval or broadly strap-shaped, narrowed towards the tip, but some, especially those with upward-facing cup-

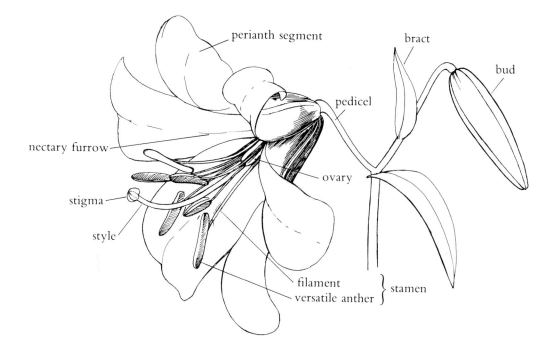

Parts of a lily flower

shaped flowers, have the segments narrowed at the base into a 'claw' which may be only just wider than the nectary furrow.

Lily flowers have six stamens, with long, slender filaments to which the pollen-bearing anthers are attached at their centres (see illustration above). Such anthers move easily backwards and forwards when touched by a visiting insect and are called 'versatile'. Many lilies have anthers of a colour that contrasts with that of the segments. Occasionally the colour of the anthers is different from that of the pollen; *L. taliense*, for example, has mauve or greyish anthers containing yellow pollen. Indeed, so much pollen is produced that the anthers are often removed from cut flowers to prevent the pollen from discolouring the petals and the table or other surface on which the flower arrangement stands.

In the centre of the flower is an ovary and a (usually three-lobed) green, whitish or purple stigma. The two are connected by a single style, which is normally long and slender, and generally longer than the stamens.

After fertilization the segments wither and fall and the ovary enlarges, eventually forming a fruit capsule, which when ripe splits open to reveal the flat seeds.

The shape of the flower

This varies enormously. It is determined by the degree of curvature of the segments (see illustration on page 26). Bell-shaped flowers (e.g. *L. nanum*) have segments that are straight or incurved towards the tips. Bowl-shaped flowers

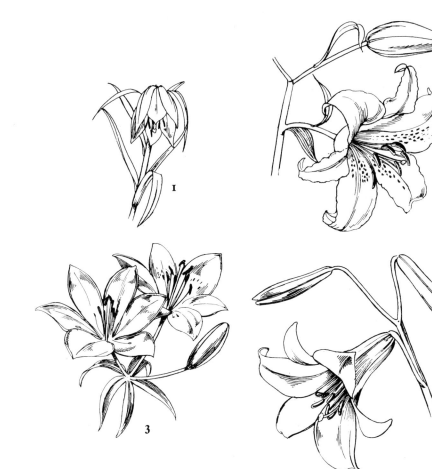

Types of flowers
1. Bell-shaped – *Lilium oxypetalum*
2. Bowl-shaped – *Lilium auratum*
3. Cup-shaped – *Lilium bulbiferum*
4. Funnel-shaped – 'Limelight'
5. Turk's-cap – *Lilium martagon*

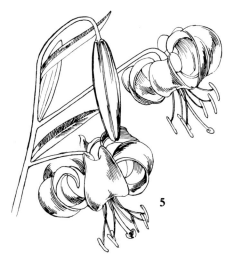

have widely spaced segments that are gradually recurved at the ends (e.g. *L. auratum*). The segments of cup-shaped or star-shaped flowers (e.g. *L. bulbiferum*) spread a little less widely than those of bowl-shaped flowers, and may or may not be recurved at the tips. Funnel-shaped flowers (e.g. *L. regale*) have the segments overlapping for most of their length and recurved or reflexed at the tips, thus forming a tubular shape that expands towards the mouth. Trumpet-shaped flowers (e.g. *L. longiflorum*) are relatively longer and narrower. Flowers of the turk's-cap or martagon type have segments that are more reflexed than in the other types, but vary in the degree of reflexion. In *L. monadelphum*, for example, they are only reflexed in the upper half, whereas in *L. pumilum* they reflex tightly for almost three-quarters of their length, producing a flower in the form of a ball.

Arrangement of flowers

The way in which the lily bears its flowers depends largely on how the flower stalks or pedicels are disposed. Those lilies that are considered by many to be especially elegant usually have long, slender pedicels. There is variation not only

Lilium martagon, a long-cultivated and long-lived species which will thrive in dappled shade (see also page 84)

in length but also in the angle at which the pedicel comes off the stem and whether or not it is straight. The combination of the shape assumed by the pedicel and the angle at which the flower is attached determines whether the flower faces upwards, downwards or outwards. The way the flower faces is an important feature and is used in the horticultural classification (see page 73).

There is also variation in the number of flowers produced by a lily plant. Most bear several flowers, but some species, such as *L. nanum*, produce only one, whereas others may have 50 or more – for example *L. martagon* and *L. humboldtii*. They can be carried in a raceme, as in *L. martagon* and *L. davidii*; a compound raceme, with two or more flowers on each pedicel, as in *L. lancifolium* and *L. henryi*, or in an umbel, as in *L. regale* and *L. sargentiae*. The size of the flowers also varies between species. The flowers of *L. pumilum*, for example, are about 3 cm (just over 1 in) across, but those of *L. auratum* can be 30 cm (12 in) across.

It is possible to have a lily with flowers of almost any colour except blue. There are lilies with flowers of a single colour, and lilies with flowers spotted or flushed with another colour. In many of the funnel-shaped flowers the segments are differently coloured on the inside and the outside.

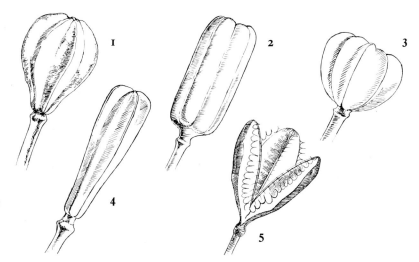

Types of fruit capsules
1. *Lilium candidum*
2. *Lilium superbum*
3. *Lilium hansonii*
4. *Lilium formosanum*
5. *Cardiocrinum giganteum*

FRUIT CAPSULES

The fruit capsule has three internal compartments, which contain the seeds stacked vertically rather like piles of pennies. When the capsule is ripe it splits open and the seeds are released. The seeds are flattened, and each has a peripheral wing; wind is the usual agent by which they are dispersed. Fruit capsules vary in shape (see above), but are characteristic for a particular species or hybrid.

The fruit capsules of species of *Cardiocrinum* are especially attractive with their toothed edges, and they can be used in indoor arrangements of dried plants.

FALSE LILIES

There are perhaps 70 or 80 plants whose common name includes the word 'lily'. Not all of these belong to the lily family (Liliaceae). They belong to a number of other families.

In the Agavaceae there is *Cordyline australis*, the palm lily; in the Amaryllidaceae there are several genera: *Crinum* species, the swamp lily, *Haemanthus* species, the fireball lilies and *Nerine sarniensis*, the Guernsey lily; in the Araceae we find *Sauromatum venosum*, the voodoo lily, *Arum* species and *Zantedeschia* species, commonly known as the arum lilies; the Asphodelaceae offer *Eremurus* species, the foxtail lilies; in the Commelinaceae there is *Tradescantia spathacea*, the boat lily; in the Convallariaceae is the sweet-smelling *Convallaria majalis*, lily of the valley; the Funkiaceae include *Hosta* species, the plantain lily; in the Hemerocallidaceae we find *Hemerocallis* species, day lilies; in the Hyacinthaceae are *Eucomis* species, the pineapple lilies; the Nymphaceae contain *Nymphaea* species, the water lilies; in the Orchidaceae is included *Calanthe triplicata*, the scrub lily; in the Ranunculaceae we find *Ranunculus lyalli*, Mount Cook lily; and in the family Xanthorrhoeaceae is *Calectasia cyanea*, the blue tinsel lily.

Within the lily family are genera other than *Lilium*, such as *Erythronium* species, the trout or fawn lilies, and *Calochortus* species, the mariposa lilies; most noteworthy, and closest to *Lilium*, are the giant Himalayan lilies of the genus *Cardiocrinum*.

Cardiocrinum

It would not be an exaggeration to say that the giant Himalayan lilies are some of the most spectacular and dramatic of all the plants you can grow in your garden. The beautiful, large white flowers never fail to attract attention.

The genus *Cardiocrinum* has three species, two of which are cultivated. For some years they were included in the genus *Lilium* but are now considered to be different enough from lilies to be put into a separate genus. They differ from true lilies in three ways. First, after the plants have flowered, the bulb dies. This is not always the end of the plant, as offset bulbs are usually produced around the parent bulb. Second, there are basal leaves in a rosette at the bottom of the stem that have long stalks and a heart-shaped leaf blade. There are also stem leaves, which decrease in size towards the top of the stem. Lastly, the fruit capsule splits open when ripe into three parts, the edges of which are attractively margined with membranous teeth. As previously mentioned, the capsules of the true lilies do not have toothed edges (see opposite).

3
Lilies in the Wild and in the Garden

One of the best features of the genus *Lilium* is that it contains species (and, indeed, cultivars) which will grow in almost any position in the garden. Much of this has to do with the natural distribution of species within the temperate zone of the northern hemisphere.

DISTRIBUTION OF LILIES IN THE WILD

There are no species of *Lilium* in the southern hemisphere, but in the northern hemisphere lilies are found in all continents. With one or two exceptions they are plants of the temperate zone. They range from North America to Europe, through Asia Minor, the Himalaya and Siberia, to China and Japan. Within this range are areas where there is a concentration of species, for example in California and Oregon in the USA, and in China with one 'outgrowth' along the Himalaya, another reaching north into Korea and Siberia, and a third embracing Kamchatka and Japan. Other smaller centres of species occur in the Caucasus and the Balkans.

Opposite: The popular *Lilium regale* (see page 89) which can be relied upon to produce its very fragrant flowers, here growing with *Nicotiana* 'Lime Green'

Left: *Lilium monadelphum*, growing among shrubs in Soviet Armenia (see also page 85)

However, even in areas where lilies are concentrated they are not exactly a major part of the vegetation – in fact they are comparatively rare.

The most northerly point reached by a lily is in Siberia, where a form of *L. martagon* grows; the southern record is held by *L. wallichianum* var. *neilgherrense*, which is isolated in the Nilgiri Hills of southern India. The lily with the most extensive natural range is *L. martagon*, which stretches from Western Europe to the Lena River in Siberia, and has to adapt to varying climates. In general, however, lily species have much smaller distributions, and some of them are restricted to tiny areas – such as *L. hansonii*, found only on an island off the South Korean coast, or *L. pitkinense*, which occurs in one area of marsh in California.

In the wild the habitats of lily species vary from woodland to meadow, and from shrub-covered stony hillsides to marsh and swamp. They are not found in very dry places, nor at very high altitude.

It would be convenient for the botanist who classifies lilies if all those with similarly shaped flowers came from the same geographical area. Unfortunately this does not happen, and flowers of all shapes are found in all continents. However, if the bulbs are considered, then it is found that most lilies with stoloniferous or rhizomatous bulbs are native to North America.

Most lilies exhibit the typical behaviour of bulbous plants, which produce leaves in the spring, flower, form seeds in the autumn and then die down, overwintering as the underground bulb. An exception to this pattern is *L. candidum*, which puts out basal leaves in the autumn that remain through the winter. It flowers in the summer and, having fruited (though it does so only rarely in cultivation) it dies back, undergoing a period of dormancy until the autumn, when the cycle begins again.

GROWING LILIES IN THE GARDEN

From the account of lilies growing in the wild it becomes apparent, and has been proved in practice, that there are lilies that can be planted in full sun or shade, in dampish or drier soil conditions, in mild areas or cold, and in soils that are acid or alkaline. They thrive in herbaceous or mixed borders, among shrubs, in dappled shade under trees, in a rock garden or in tubs on the patio. Some lilies are easy to grow and suitable for the beginner, others will test the patience and expertise of the specialist.

The vast majority of lilies produce their flowers in mid summer; a lesser number flower in early summer, or in late summer to early autumn. It is therefore possible to have lilies in flower for almost six months each year.

The number of lilies you can plant in your garden obviously depends on the size of the garden (and on the size of your pocket). Drifts of lilies look wonderful, but are only for those whose gardens are large. In smaller gardens lilies will probably be planted in small groups, often of less than half a dozen plants. When planting in small numbers, it looks better if the lilies are planted in threes, fives or sevens; twos, fours and sixes do not seem to work as well. The bulbs should be sensibly arranged in a group, not planted in a straight row. Above seven, the actual number in the group becomes less important. This advice on numbers applies not only to lilies but also to all other bulbous or herbaceous plants.

Many lilies are rather expensive to buy, and it may be that the gardener will only be able to afford a single bulb. However, with a little patience, it is soon possible to build up the stock by means of propagation by scales (see pages 58–60).

When planting in groups it is better not to mix the species or cultivars together. A clump that contains more than one kind of lily rarely looks attractive. Groups of some of the variable grexes, however, which may contain plants with flowers of various colours, are acceptable.

The height to which a lily grows must obviously be considered when deciding where to place it. Many lilies, such as *L. monadelphum* or the Mid-Century Hybrids, look lovely in a herbaceous border, and it is only common sense to plant the short lilies near the front and the tall ones further back. The tall lilies in particular, such as *L. pardalinum* var. *giganteum* or *L. auratum*, benefit from being planted among plants of similar size which will act as protection from strong winds. Examples of suitable companions include *Ligularia stenocephala* 'The Rocket' or *Ligularia* 'Gregynog Gold', *Inula magnifica*, the taller heleniums, or tall grasses such as the impressive *Miscanthus sacchariflorus* and *M. sinensis*.

No lilies like to be planted in a position where they will be subjected to a lot of wind. Lilies do not look very nice if they have to be staked, though it may be necessary if the stems are fairly slender and carry a lot of flowers, like *L. davidii* var. *willmottiae*. It is worth finding a fairly sheltered spot in which to grow them. On the other hand, a place where they will receive light breezes is actually beneficial as the risk of fungal infection will be reduced.

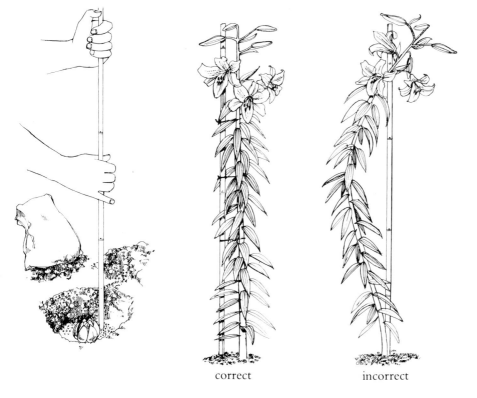

correct   incorrect

It is best to insert the stake when the bulb is planted to avoid later root damage. As the stem grows it should be attached to the stake at regular intervals so the entire length is supported

Opposite: *Lilium davidii* comes from China and produces numerous bulblets at the base of the flowering stem, just below ground level (see also page 79)

Right: *Lilium pardalinum* is one of the tallest American species (see page 87). The large spots give it the name of leopard lily

LILIES AND SHRUBS

Planting lilies among shrubs is a good idea, not only because the shrubs offer protection but because the lilies usually bloom after the shrubs have finished flowering. Many shrubs produce their flowers in the spring or early summer, and when they have finished flowering look rather dull. Rhododendrons and azaleas are obvious examples; forsythia, camellias, witch hazel, mahonia, philadelphus and some viburnums are others. Lilies planted near these shrubs will brighten the rather dreary foliage; yellow and white lilies such as *L. auratum*, Sentinel Strain or Copper King Strain are especially effective. Some of the tall lilies with red and orange flowers, such as *L. pardalinum* or 'Viking', can also look very striking planted among shrubs.

A further advantage of planting lilies with shrubs is that the shrubs can act as a barrier to pests and diseases. When a clump of lilies becomes infected with a virus disease there is a great danger that aphids will carry the virus to nearby plants. However, the aphids will often be prevented from reaching neighbouring lilies if there is an obstructing shrub.

THE WOODLAND GARDEN

Lilies can be beautiful in a woodland setting, and there are several species and hybrids to choose from that will grow happily in semi-shade. *L. martagon* often grows in woodland glades in the wild, and in the garden the various colour forms can provide pretty splashes of colour, especially when lit up by dappled sunlight.

Dense tree cover will not provide a suitable environment for lilies, but lighter shade, like that given by birches or some species of *Prunus*, is ideal for lilies that prefer some shade. Lilies also associate well with the Japanese maples, *Acer japonicum* and *A. palmatum* and their numerous cultivars. For a really spectacular display, try cardiocrinums in a woodland setting. Apart from the fact that *Cardiocrinum* is one of the best neighbour-impressing plants you can grow, these wonderful, tall, white-trumpeted lilies will provide an unforgettable sight. They are particularly suited to a woodland garden where the conditions match the dank mountain woodland of their native homes. There is a fine planting at Wakehurst Place in Sussex, Kew's country home, where they grow better than at Kew with its lighter soils and lower rainfall.

ROCK GARDENS AND RAISED BEDS

Most lilies are too tall for a rock garden, but a few are dwarf enough, and carefully sited will look delightful. Those whose gardening activities are limited to rock gardens need not feel that they cannot grow lilies. Two eminently suitable lilies, *L. nanum* and *L. oxypetalum*, rarely exceed 45 cm (18 in) and are usually less. *L. pomponium*, with its scarlet turk's-cap flowers borne on slender stems, is another species worth trying.

Lilies are ideal for a raised bed, and a raised bed is ideal for lilies because the drainage is deliberately sharp. A small raised bed can usually be constructed in even the tiniest garden.

The low plants often grown in a rock garden can provide useful ground cover, which will help to shade the lily bulbs from strong sun. Lilies will be perfectly happy growing through mat-forming plants such as thyme, aubrieta, small species of *Dianthus*, or some of the dwarf phloxes.

LILIES IN CONTAINERS

A really small garden may limit the growing of lilies to pots or tubs. An advantage in using containers is that they can be moved around as needed. While the lilies are growing the pots can be put somewhere inconspicuous, and then, as the lilies burst into bloom, the pots can be given a prominent position. The recent increase in popularity of the terrace or patio means that many gardens now boast a paved area, and this provides an excellent setting for container-grown plants.

Having said that pots and tubs can be moved around, it must nevertheless be remembered that very large containers, once they have been filled with the growing medium, will in fact be too heavy to move unless one has a team of strong men at one's disposal! So if you are planting up a really large pot or tub, make sure that it is in its final position before you put the compost into it.

Terracotta pots are among the most attractive containers for growing lilies as the colour is sympathetic. They are now available in a wide range of styles and at a variety of prices to suit all purses. Wooden tubs or half-barrels are also pleasing to the eye. In a modern setting, where concrete or reconstituted stone have been used, containers made of such materials do not look out of place, whereas they can jar in more traditional garden surroundings. The choice of containers is as

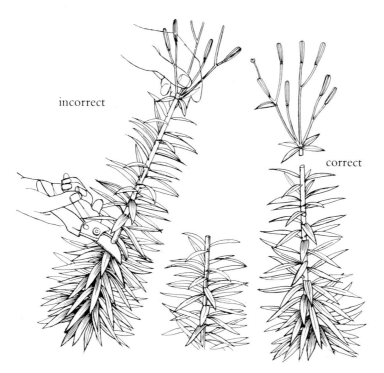

incorrect

correct

Old flower heads should be cut off as soon as the flowers have withered. It is a mistake to remove any but the topmost leaves, as the leaves are needed to make food for next year's growth.

personal as the choice of plants; it is wise to consider the options carefully before buying in order to avoid spending a lot of money on a purchase that may later be regretted.

It is particularly desirable to remove regularly faded blooms from plants growing in containers to keep the display at its best. Lilies in containers can look very striking planted on their own with nothing to detract from their beauty. Small companion plants, however, help to keep the bulbs cool by shading the soil, and can add a contrasting or similar colour as desired.

Companion plants

Annuals are particularly useful for this purpose, and should be sown directly into the soil of the container in the spring. For example, the orange Californian poppy, *Eschscholtzia californica*, can look startling with white lilies; blue love-in-a-mist, *Nigella damascena*, is pretty with pink or orange lilies.

White daisies are lovely companions for lilies, and in pots or tubs *Chrysanthemum frutescens* (now correctly called *Argyranthemum frutescens*) is ideal. It is widely available from nurseries and garden centres. Another recommended daisy is *Chrysanthemum multicaule* 'Gold Plate', which has rather succulent dissected leaves and cheerful flowers of bright yellow; it can be purchased as a bedding plant. Some of the newer developments in the hybrids of *Gazania* are worth considering, such as 'Chansonette', 'Mini Star' and 'Sundance'. South African in origin, gazanias produce large daisy-type flowers in bright colours, and often have a white-centered black eye at the base of each 'petal' – a most attractive feature. 'Chansonette' comes in a range of colours from yellow or orange to brownish or pinkish, and will grow to about 23 cm (9 in) tall; 'Mini Star' produces compact plants of about the same height and is also available in a

mixture of colours, or in yellow or tangerine only; 'Sundance' is a taller plant, up to 30 cm (1 ft) tall, with a lax habit and long-stalked flowers that can measure as much as 13 cm (5 in) in diameter. The range of colours tends to be darker than that of the other cultivars – orange or reddish brown, or sometimes red and yellow striped. There is a silver-leaved *Gazania* called 'Carnival', which again offers a variety of colours, including pink, orange and reddish brown. Gazanias are not hardy in cooler areas, but can be overwintered as cuttings; taking cuttings enables the gardener to choose the flower colours he prefers.

Trailing plants can be used to great effect in containers (even the trailing cultivars of the ubiquitous annual *Lobelia*). Ivy-leaved pelargoniums are now available in colours ranging from white through pink to red or lilac, or even two-tone flowers. *Verbena* 'Springtime' is a trailing, free-flowering verbena with heads of flowers in white, pink, red, mauve or purple. Obviously, to plant this with orange lilies would be considered by most people to be misguided or daring! *Helichrysum petiolare* is a most useful trailer whose pale, grey-green leaves will soon disguise a container that is less than beautiful. It is now also available as a cultivar with yellowish leaves, called 'Limelight'.

Other useful grey-leaved plants include *Senecio bicolor* subsp. *cineraria* in its selections 'Silverdust' and 'Diamond'. (These plants will usually be found in

Opposite: *Lilium superbum* is a tall species with scented flowers which are produced towards the end of the lily season (see also page 92)

Left: A mixed border in which deep yellow lilies have been planted with the brownish purple-leaved *Cimicifuga* 'Brunette', a purple-leaved *Berberis* and catmint

catalogues and garden centres under the names *Senecio cineraria* or *Cineraria maritima*, despite the fact that these names have long been superseded.) *Pyrethrum (Achillea) ptarmicaefolium* is another silver-leaved plant that can be planted in a container with lilies. Grey or silver leaves have a cooling effect on hot-coloured lilies such as 'Enchantment' or *L. pumilum*.

PLANTS TO GROW WITH LILIES

Lilies are wonderful plants for a herbaceous or mixed border, but it must be remembered that some companion plants are actually too competitive, and the lilies will not grow successfully if planted too close to them. Peonies, for example, are very greedy feeders and will rob the lily roots of the nutrients they require.

Colour combination in the garden is a very personal choice. Many books have been written on the subject, some of the most famous being by the English garden designer, Gertrude Jekyll. Out of print for many years, her books have now been reprinted and make fascinating reading.

Lilies come in all colours except blue, so there is plenty of choice. The choice is increased by the variation in the shape of the flowers. Lilies can be chosen to match the surrounding flowers or to contrast with them. Obviously the flowering times of the lilies and their associated plants must also be considered when you are making your selection.

White lilies are especially useful for planting near plants with very bright flowers. They can be used to 'cool' an area of hot or strident colour. *L. regale* is particularly recommended as it is so easy to grow. It looks wonderful planted next to blue agapanthus or delphiniums. Perhaps surprisingly, white lilies are very effective when planted with grey- or silver-leaved plants such as santolinas, artemisias or *Senecio* 'Sunshine'.

Conversely, plants with white or cream flowers are very useful to complement lilies with really brilliant flowers. There are so many available that any choice must be personal. White agapanthus are always a good standby, as are white or cream roses, *Tradescantia virginiana* 'Osprey', white foxgloves or some of the white-flowered hebes.

It is worth experimenting with unusual colour combinations. If you do not like the results, the lilies can easily be moved in the autumn. Lilies with bright orange flowers can be planted next to yellow-leaved shrubs such as *Philadelphus coronarius* 'Aureus', *Sambucus nigra* 'Aurea' or one of the smaller conifers with yellow foliage. Orange and purple can give an exciting and somewhat unorthodox effect – try orange lilies against a purple-leaved *Cotinus coggygria* such as 'Royal Purple' or 'Notcutt's Variety', the purple hazel, *Corylus maxima* 'Purpurea', or one of the Japanese maples such as *Acer palmatum* 'Dissectum Atropurpureum'. Purple-leaved plants also associate well with red- and yellow-flowered lilies.

Blue conifers or the blue-green leaves of *Eucalyptus gunnii* (kept to a manageable height by pruning) make a lovely background for lilies of various colours – red or orange can be spectacular, while pink or pale yellow give a softer effect.

Pink and blue are colours that have always been used together in gardens. Combinations of pink lilies with blue campanulas, eryngiums or echinops and with pink foxgloves or Japanese anemones give a cottage garden feeling. Roses and lilies are old friends, and all sorts of schemes are possible, using either old roses or some of the modern, often more garish cultivars.

Smaller plants that associate well with lilies include pinks, catmint, lavender, *Anaphalis nubigena* or *A. triplinervis*, some of the more dwarf geraniums such as *G. ibericum* or *G. wallichianum*, and *Scabiosa* 'Butterfly Blue'. Some of the smaller-flowered violas, such as *V. cornuta*, *V.* 'Maggie Mott' or 'Bowles's Black' also look most effective.

The various species and cultivars of *Hosta* that are now so popular can provide light relief with their beautiful sculptural leaves, which come in various shades of green, yellowish or bluish. The green theme can be extended by the use of ferns. *Matteuccia struthiopteris*, the shuttlecock or ostrich plume fern, is a fine companion for the taller lilies. Smaller ferns include *Dryopteris filix-mas*, the male fern, *Adiantum pedatum* from North America, with its prettily shaped fronds, the delicate-looking *Cystopteris fragilis*, and species of *Polystichum*. There are many more to choose from – consult books or friends, or visit a nursery or garden centre that sells hardy ferns. 'Hardy' should be stressed here, as there are many ferns sold as pot-plants that will not survive a winter out of doors.

The possibilities and plant associations are endless, and could make a book all on their own. Perhaps the best advice is to use your eyes. Note what is growing in the gardens of friends and neighbours. Visit garden centres and nurseries and send for catalogues to find out what is for sale. Visit some of the many gardens, both large and small, that are open to the public. Read some of the myriad gardening books now available. Adopt any ideas you find attractive to use in your own garden, and then sit back and wait for the compliments.

4
Cultivation

It is important to start with healthy bulbs. When lily bulbs are purchased from garden centres or retail bulb companies, they often arrive dried out and possibly diseased. They may have been out of the soil for several weeks or even months. The lack of the bulb-coat that bulbs of most other genera possess means that lily bulbs dry out rather more quickly than, for example, tulips or daffodils.

BEFORE PLANTING

When lily bulbs are received they should be carefully examined. Before planting, any desiccation or disease must be attended to. Any scales showing signs of fungal attack must be removed and destroyed by burning, or put into a polythene bag or wrapped in newspaper and disposed of. The bulb should then be immersed for a couple of hours in a solution of a systemic fungicide such as benomyl. If the bulbs have been out of the ground for some time they should be placed in damp peat for about two weeks in a cool, frost-free place such as a garage, cellar or garden shed (at about 6–8°C/43–46°F) until they become plumper and firmer and even show signs of producing roots. If outdoor conditions permit, the bulbs should then be planted in the garden; if it is too cold they should be put into large pots and grown under glass or other suitable protection.

Choice of site in the garden
Most lilies like a sunny position in the garden, but there are exceptions, and some species and hybrids actually prefer a shady site. Even lilies that are sun-lovers grow better if their roots are shaded.

PLANTING

Lily bulbs can be planted at any time of the year warm enough to allow active growth – in other words, any time but mid winter. Never attempt to plant bulbs in frozen ground. Apart from the physical difficulty of digging hard soil, the bulb will simply sit in the cold ground and run the risk of rotting.

Bulbs that have stem roots should be planted more deeply than those that do not produce them. This is why stem roots are mentioned in the descriptions of lilies in the A to Z section of this book (see page 74 ff.). Stem-rooting lilies like to have plenty of soil above the bulb, into which the stem roots can penetrate and feed. The bulbs should generally be planted at a depth about two and a half times the height of the bulb. Thus a bulb that measures 4 cm (2½ in) from base to tip should be planted with the tip at a depth of 10 cm (4 in).

A few lilies prefer to be planted quite shallowly. *L. candidum* and its hybrid *L.* × *testaceum* grow best when they have the tops of their bulbs almost at soil level.

While the bulbs are being planted their position should be marked with a small stick or cane. It is dangerous to wait until the leaves emerge from the soil, for a

Opposite: 'Marhan' growing happily among shrubs in a semi-shady part of the garden (see also page 106)

marker inserted at this stage may pierce and cause damage to the bulb.

Newly planted lilies, especially in colder areas, should be covered with dead bracken or peat during the winter. This helps to give some protection from hard frosts. The covering should be removed in spring as the weather begins to warm up. To prevent the bracken blowing away in winter storms, it can be weighed down with some soil, or fixed with wire netting, the edges of which are pushed into the flowerbed.

The bulbs of lilies producing stem roots should be covered with soil to approximately two and half times their depth

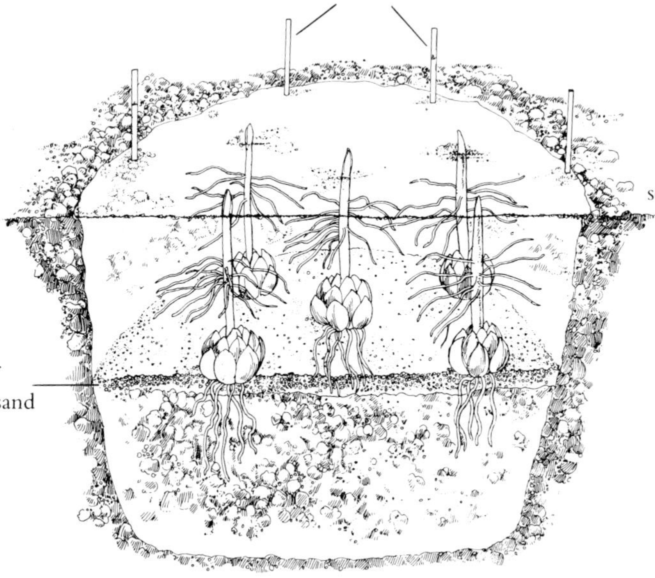

position of bulbs marked with small sticks

soil level

bed of sharp sand

soil cultivated to two spades depth

position of bulb marked with stick

soil level

bed of sharp sand

Lilium candidum is an example of a lily which does not produce stem roots and likes to be shallowly planted

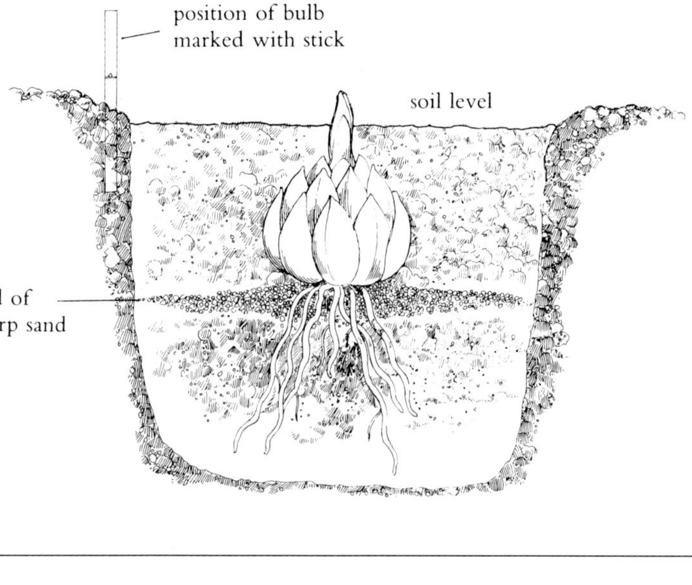

Cardiocrinums

These plants grow best in semi-shady conditions. The soil must be fairly rich and contain a lot of leafmould. A woodland garden is ideal. An application of fertilizer in the spring is a good idea, and there should be plenty of water in the growing season. The bulbs must not be planted too deeply. The tip of the bulb should be level with the surface of the ground, with the 'nose' almost emerging. In cooler areas the bulbs should be covered with a mulch of leaves or bracken to protect them from cold. Bulbs should be planted about 1 m (3 ft) apart; if they are planted too close to one another the mature flowering plants will be overcrowded.

REPLANTING

It may become necessary to replant lilies, either because they are in an unsuitable place or because the bulbs have increased so much they have become overcrowded. Some gardeners move their bulbs immediately after flowering has finished, while the leaves are still green. At this time the roots are still active, so the bulb should settle into its new position without a setback. However, the leaves on the long stem will lose water rapidly and will tend to wilt rather badly until the roots are established. Other gardeners wait until the autumn, when the stem has withered, and the bulb has fattened up ready for the next season.

There is no real advantage to moving bulbs at either time. The gardener should choose the time that is most convenient and fits in with other garden jobs. The only time bulbs should not be moved is during the winter when the soil is very cold or even frozen. Whenever the bulbs are moved, care must be taken to ensure that the roots are not damaged.

DRAINAGE AND SOIL

Good drainage is perhaps the most important factor in lily-growing. Lilies must have a well-drained soil – excessive moisture in the soil will result in deterioration, rot and eventual death of the bulb. Some species, such as *L. pardalinum* and *L. superbum*, are found in wettish conditions in their native habitats, even growing in marshy ground or swamps, but if these conditions are imitated in the garden, the plants will die!

If your soil is heavy, with a high clay content, then steps must be taken to open it up by the addition of well-rotted compost or manure and grit or coarse sand. The ideal soil for most lilies (though there are some exceptions) has plenty of humus but drains freely.

Most lilies need a good depth of soil, so there is little point in improving only the top layer. A bulb that is planted in well-worked topsoil will not appreciate its roots growing down into unsuitable, badly drained subsoil. Soil where lilies are to be planted should preferably have been double-dug – i.e. dug down to two spade-depths.

Some gardeners plant their bulbs on a bed of sharp sand to help free drainage, and surround the bulbs with some sharp sand which is usually successful in discouraging slugs. Certainly slugs tend to avoid sand and grit because they find it difficult to move over the angular surface.

If your garden slopes it is likely to be well drained. If part of the garden slopes, try planting lilies on the sloping areas.

The great majority of lilies prefer an acid or neutral soil, but there are exceptions. There are lilies that will tolerate alkalinity, but a few lilies, such as *L. henryi*, will only grow in an alkaline soil, i.e. one with a pH higher than 7, due to its lime content. Conversely, a few lilies, for example *L. auratum* and *L. speciosum*, require an acid soil. Special soil requirements are mentioned where necessary under particular lilies in the A to Z section.

WATERING

Despite demanding good drainage, lilies do not appreciate a drought. In particular, they like to have plenty of moisture while they are growing, up to the time when they flower. It may be necessary, especially if you live in an area where the rainfall is unpredictable, to provide supplementary water. When watering either with a hose or a watering can, take care not to wet the leaves of the lilies. The more the leaves are wetted, the more likely they are to succumb to disease. It is best to direct the water at the roots of the plants, where it will do the most good. Watering will be most effective if the soil surface is not allowed to become so dry and hard that water runs off it rather than sinking in.

In drier regions where the summer rainfall is generally inadequate for lilies it

Pink Pearl Trumpets whose scented flowers give a delightful display well into late summer (see also page 109)

may be sensible to set up a permanent system of trickle irrigation. The pipes that supply the water can be disguised by the careful use of suitable plants. Insufficient water while lilies are actively growing will often result in stunted plants with diminished resistance to pests and diseases.

In areas where the tap water is hard, make sure that lime-hating lilies are watered only with collected rainwater (unless you have a water softener).

FEEDING

Lilies appreciate feeding in the growing season; either a liquid feed or a general granulated fertilizer containing nitrogen, phosphorus and potassium in equal parts can be used. In the latter case, the rain or artificial watering will gradually wash the nutrients down into the soil. Fresh farmyard manure must never be applied in case it damages the bulbs, but well-rotted manure is fine. Feeding will help the lily to make good large bulbs for the following year.

Stem-rooting lilies that have not been planted deeply enough should be mulched with soil containing a generous amount of leafmould as soon as stem roots are seen.

AUTUMN CARE AND WINTER PROTECTION

Unless seed is required for propagation, the dead flowers should be cut off once flowering is over (see page 37), so that the plant does not put unnecessary energy into seed production. In autumn, after the stem has withered, it should be removed by pulling or twisting it off, and burned or otherwise destroyed, together with any old leaves that may be lying on the ground. This is to prevent the dead remains harbouring any diseases through the winter. It is worth dusting the hole left by the stem with a fungicidal powder containing quintozene or carbendazin, and adding a sprinkling of grit or coarse sand as a discouragement to slugs (see page 64). A mulch of leafmould or even pine needles will help to protect the bulbs when hard frosts arrive.

LILIES IN CONTAINERS

Lilies grown in pots should not be left outside over the winter. In the open ground lily bulbs are usually sited below the level to which frost penetrates, but in a pot the soil may freeze from the sides. The container should be stored in a frost-free shed or garage, but there must be no heat in case the bulbs start to grow early. If space in the garden permits, the pot can be plunged in a sheltered place and covered with bracken or peat for protection. In the spring, once all danger of frost is past, the pots can be dug up. Burying is, however, unsuitable for pots or containers that are especially decorative.

Any large containers can be used provided that they are deep enough for the lily roots – at least 30 cm (1 ft) should be allowed. As in the open garden, drainage is of paramount importance, particularly if the container is plastic. Plastic pots do not dry out as rapidly as those made of clay, and a plastic pot filled with heavy soil and subjected to a lengthy period of rain will be very soggy inside. In such conditions lily bulbs will rot.

The autumn is the best time to plant lilies in pots or tubs, if the bulbs can be obtained by then. Spring planting is often necessary, however, because that is when the bulbs may arrive from the retailer. The most suitable compost for containers is John Innes No. 2 or 3, with added grit and leafmould. The bottom of the container should be covered with a layer of bracken, crocks or gravel, followed by a layer of leafmould or well-rotted manure. The compost is then added and the bulbs are planted. The number of bulbs planted in a container depends on both the size of the container and the size of the bulbs. In general the bulbs should be planted about halfway down the container, and covered with 5–8 cm (2–3 in) of compost. The container should then be well watered so that the compost settles closely around each bulb. Further water should only be given if the compost begins to dry out.

When the lilies begin to grow in the spring more water will be needed. The compost must never become dry, nor must it be too wet, so careful watering is necessary. Pots containing stem-rooting lilies may need to be topped up with extra compost if stem-roots are produced above soil level. Because the amount of compost is limited, it is important to feed lilies grown in containers. A liquid feed can be given every two weeks, or a slow-release granular fertilizer applied about once a month.

A further advantage of a container is that the gardener has complete control over the compost. Lilies that hate lime, such as *L. auratum* and *L. speciosum*, cannot be grown in a garden with limy soil, but they can be grown in containers; use lime-free compost, and make sure that you do not water them with hard water.

Lilies grown in small containers should be repotted every year; in large containers every second year will suffice. This is best done in late autumn when the stems and leaves have withered. Care must be taken when repotting not to damage the roots.

LILIES AS CUT FLOWERS

Lilies make beautiful and often long-lasting cut flowers. Gardeners who cut lilies usually have quite a number of plants out of doors, and the odd stem taken into the house is not missed. To cut the entire length of the stem will weaken the plant, which may not produce flowers the following year. It is therefore better to cut only about half the stem, leaving the bottom half of the leafy stem to continue to manufacture food that will be stored in the bulb.

The best time to cut lilies is when the first flower on the stem is beginning to open. The other flowers will open successively in water. As with most cut flowers, the leaves should be stripped from the part of the stem in the water, or they will rot and make the water smell unpleasant.

LILIES UNDER GLASS

A greenhouse will enable the gardener to have lilies in flower before their natural blooming time. The lilies most often forced commercially are *L. longiflorum*, *L. speciosum* and some of the Asiatic Hybrids; these are the lilies that commonly appear in florist's shops.

The other major advantage of a greenhouse is to be able to grow species and cultivars that are too tender to be grown outdoors in all but the warmest areas, and so need glass protection – for example, *L. wallichianum*, *L. philippinense* and *L. catesbaei*.

Large pots are fine for the cultivation of lilies in a greenhouse, but lilies with a stoloniform habit (see pages 21 and 23), such as *L. nepalense* or *L. wallichianum*, are unsuitable for pot culture. They are better grown in a greenhouse bed or border if one can be provided.

In order to have lilies in flower earlier than their normal flowering time, the bulbs can either be planted under glass in the autumn, or they can be dug up from the garden in January (provided the ground is not frozen) and potted up. The compost used should be composed of 7 parts sterilized loam, 3 parts peat and 2 parts sharp sand; extra grit and leafmould or other humus should be added to this mixture. A general fertilizer such as Growmore should be used according to the instructions given on the bag. The compost can be modified to suit lilies with special requirements, such as the lime-lovers.

The temperature in the greenhouse should not be allowed to drop more than a degree or so below freezing point in winter. To produce early bulb growth, a minimum of about $8°C$ ($45°F$) should be maintained. In summer it may be difficult to prevent the greenhouse from overheating, especially in warmer regions or during hot, sunny weather. Lilies dislike being subjected to temperatures above $32°C$ ($90°F$), so steps must be taken to ensure that the temperature does not rise excessively. The importance of ventilation cannot be overstressed, not only because moving air helps to keep the temperature down but also because it reduces the risk of fungal infection. Automatic ventilators are a sensible idea for anyone who is not constantly on hand to monitor the greenhouse conditions.

Some kind of shading will probably be necessary during the summer months if the lilies are not to suffer from overheating. This also applies to most other plants. One solution is to apply a glasshouse shading wash (usually white or pale green) to the glass, which will reduce the amount of sunlight that reaches the inside of the house. There are some shading washes that are rendered less opaque in rainy conditions, and normal rain will not remove the wash from the glass. In the autumn the wash can be removed by scrubbing. However, in areas of uncertain and changeable weather, this method is less than ideal. Other methods of shading involve netting or slatted blinds, which can be rolled into position when necessary, and these are more controllable.

Pests and diseases

Control of pests under glass is very important. It is sensible to spray against aphids, for example with gamma-HCH or permethrin, before they actually put in an appearance. Good ventilation will help to prevent fungal attack, but a fungicidal spray such as one containing benomyl or carbendazin will not go amiss. If any sign of disease or pest is seen, immediate steps must be taken to combat the trouble.

5
Propagation

Most people buy their bulbs, be they tulips, daffodils, crocuses or lilies, from a shop or garden centre or by mail order from a bulb company or nurseryman. The idea of raising bulbs from seed seems at first to be rather ridiculous, mainly because of the time factor. Purchased bulbs will flower in the same or the following year, whereas raising bulbs from seed can take several years (generally between three and six) from sowing to flowering.

SEED

The reason for many lily-growers raising their plants from seed is to avoid virus diseases (see p. 68), which are not carried by the seed. Even seed collected from infected plants will be free from the virus. Virus-free stock is especially important to the enthusiast who wishes to grow many different lilies, because once plants become infected the virus can spread rapidly, disfiguring and eventually often killing the lilies.

Another advantage of using seed is the greater choice of species and hybrids that is available. The range of lilies offered by nurseries or garden centres as flowering-size bulbs is restricted, though it does tend to vary from year to year. A glance at the seed list of a specialist society will reveal a far greater number of lilies, some of which may be unnamed seedlings that growers have produced in experiments in hybridizing. Some of the rarer species of lilies may be available only as seed.

Now that conservation of lilies in the wild is so important and the digging up of bulbs is prohibited, judicious collection of seed is a way of bringing new material into cultivation.

Finally, the purchase of seed should be considered if money is a limiting factor, as it is considerably cheaper than buying bulbs.

Seed of a clone (see p. 72) should not be used, for the sexual progeny of such a parent will exhibit variation and the seedlings will not be 'true' to the clone. When two plants cross, the progeny normally possess some of the characteristics of each parent. By definition, a clone is made up of individuals all of which have the same genetic constitution, and the only way in which a member of a clone can reproduce is by vegetative means, not by seed.

Germination
Lily seeds have two types of germination, known as epigeal and hypogeal (see the illustrations on page 52).

Epigeal germination In this type of germination the cotyledon or seed leaf emerges above the surface of the soil, often with the seed coat still attached, in which case the seed coat splits and is discarded as the seed leaf expands. In some species the seed coat is left behind under the ground and the seed leaf emerges

Opposite: *Lilium parryi* is a lovely, much sought-after species from the south-western USA. It is not easy to grow and is rather susceptible to fungal diseases (see also page 87)

without it. Below ground, the tiny bulb and the roots begin to grow larger, and finally the first true leaf is produced.

Hypogeal germination In this case the seed produces a root that quickly forms a small bulb, and the cotyledon (encased in the seed coat) remains underground. When the first true leaf is formed, it breaks through the soil surface.

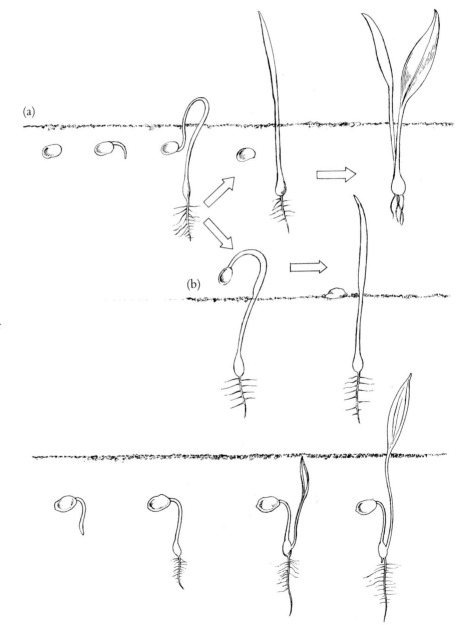

(a)

(b)

Above: Epigeal germination. The seed coat can either be left behind in the soil **(a)**, or carried above ground on the tip of the first leaf **(b)** **Below:** Hypogeal germination

Immediate or delayed Both epigeal and hypogeal germination is delayed in some species, sometimes for up to two years. It is important to remember about this delay; otherwise seeds that have apparently failed to germinate but in fact are only delayed may be thrown away.

When seed is sown, account must be taken of whether germination is immediate (two to eight weeks) or delayed (several months to two years). In general, most epigeal germination is immediate and most hypogeal germination is delayed, though there are exceptions. The various germination patterns are probably linked to the climatic conditions that the species experience in their native habitats. The time that a seed takes to germinate depends not only on its inbuilt germination type but also on the temperature at which it is kept while it is germinating.

Seed sowing

Sowing lily seeds directly into the ground out of doors is not generally recommended, though *L. regale* is an exception. Seed-raising in a greenhouse or even on a suitable windowsill is much to be preferred.

Most people sow the seeds in deep seed boxes or half pots. Either clay or plastic pots can be used. A well-drained compost, made up of 1 part sterilized loam, 2 parts peat and 2 parts sharp sand with extra coarse sand or grit added, should be used; the seed should be dusted with a fungicide containing carbendazin or quintozene.

Seed of the species with immediate germination should be sown in the autumn as soon as it is ripe, or in spring if the grower finds it difficult to maintain a temperature of about 16°C (60°F) and to provide adequate post-germination light. The lower light levels of winter can result in pale, spindly seedlings whose start in life is disadvantaged. Depending on the temperature, the seed should germinate in two to eight weeks.

All bulbs except the concentric type, can be carefully divided by breaking them apart and replanting the resultant smaller bulbs

The seed of species with delayed germination is best sown in early autumn. After four or five months the seeds need to be subjected to a temperature of about 5°C (41°F) for six weeks or so. This 'vernalization' will break the dormancy and encourage leaf growth, and is most easily achieved by placing the pots or boxes out of doors in a sheltered place, but not one where the air is stagnant.

Alternatively, seed with delayed hypogeal germination can be put into a polythene bag containing a moist (not wet) sterilized mixture of more or less equal parts of grit and peat. The seeds should be dusted with a fungicidal powder such as quintozene. The bag should be sealed and put in a warm place, about 21°C (70°F), such as an airing cupboard until the bulblets have formed. The bag is then placed somewhere very cool (the salad drawer of a refrigerator is ideal) and kept there for two or three months. The tiny plants should then be transferred to pots. It is important that they should not be potted up too early in the year, before conditions are suitable for growth; round about mid spring is the best time.

Time from seed sowing to flowering varies according to the species or hybrid – it is usually between three and six years. *L. formosanum* is exceptional in that, given good conditions, it will produce flowers in six to twelve months.

Cardiocrinum

Cardiocrinums grown from seed take six or seven years to flower, but they are well worth waiting for. If possible, it is best to sow seeds each year so that you will have a succession of flowering plants. The seeds will germinate immediately if they are sown as soon as they are ripe, but if there is any delay in sowing germination will be held up for about a year.

DIVISION

This method applies mainly to lilies with stoloniferous or rhizomatous bulbs, most of which come from North America. As the bulbs grow and branch, they can be divided by carefully breaking the smaller bulbs apart. The divisions are then replanted in the required position. This is best undertaken in the autumn, before the weather gets too chilly and growth ceases. The bulbs will have time to grow new roots before winter arrives, and in the following spring will not need to rely completely on the stored food within the bulb.

BULBILS

Some lilies, unfortunately only relatively few in number, produce bulbils in the leaf axils; examples are *L. bulbiferum*, *L. lancifolium* and *L. sargentiae*. The bulbils can be removed and planted out of doors in a prepared bed, or grown in an unheated greenhouse or frame. They should be detached from the parent plant in the autumn. If left long enough they will often produce roots while still attached to the parent. It is not essential, but it is preferable to separate and plant them before this happens, so that when the roots appear they will grow into the soil rather than being exposed to the air. After removal from the parent they should be planted immediately to prevent any desiccation.

If the bulbils are being grown on outdoors, they should be planted about 2.5 cm (1 in) deep and about 2.5 cm (1 in) apart, in rows in well-drained soil; it is

Opposite: *Lilium lancifolium* var. *splendens* is a vigorous variety of the popular tiger lily. It flowers towards the end of the lily season (see also page 81)

Some lilies produce bulbils in their leaf axils which can be carefully detached and planted in pots of well-drained compost

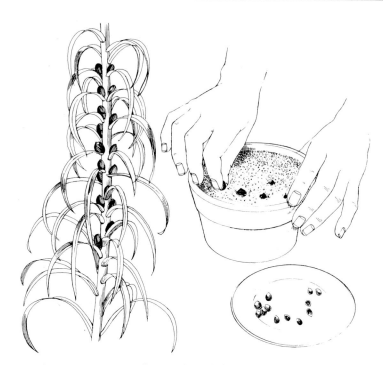

important to keep an eye open for snails and slugs and to keep the bed weed free. The bulbils can be given a general fertilizer in the growing season and normally remain in the bed for two years; they can then be moved to a permanent place in the garden.

Bulbils that are to be grown under glass should be planted about 2.5 cm (1 in) apart in pots or deep boxes of well-drained compost and placed in a frame or unheated greenhouse. It is not necessary to bury the bulbils – they can be pressed into the surface of the compost and then covered with a layer of grit. They are usually left for a year or so – in the following autumn they will be large enough to be transplanted into the garden.

It should be remembered that if the parent plant is infected with virus disease the bulbils will also be infected, and should therefore not be used for propagation.

Some lilies that do not normally produce bulbils can be induced to do so artificially by removing the flower buds just before they open. Bulbils will then develop in the leaf axils during the summer, and can be removed in the autumn and planted. Species that do this are *L. candidum*, *L. chalcedonicum*, *L. dauricum*, *L. × hollandicum*, *L. leichtlinii*, *L. maculatum* and *L. × testaceum*.

Depending on the species or hybrid involved, lily bulbils will reach flowering size in two to five years.

BULBLETS

These are produced above the parent bulb at the base of the stem, and can be detached and grown on as outlined above. They tend to occur in Asiatic lilies such as *L. auratum* and *L. lancifolium*. To encourage their formation the lilies should be mulched with a compost rich in leafmould. (Some people like to add wood ash and bonemeal.) In the autumn, when the stem has withered, the bulblets can be removed, taking care not to damage the delicate roots that will probably have been produced. Like the bulbils, they should be planted immediately in case they begin to dry out. Also like the bulbils, they can be grown on outdoors or under glass.

Artificial production

If lots of bulblets are required, lilies that produce them naturally can be artificially persuaded to produce more by the following method. The flower stem is removed from the bulb by twisting, leaving the parent bulb in the ground. Any flowers or buds are pinched out. A trench about 15 cm (6 in) deep is dug, with one end sloping upwards to the level of the soil surface. The stem is laid along the trench with the upper end protruding, and the stem and leaves are sprayed with a fungicide such as benomyl to discourage fungal infection. The trench should then be filled in with a sandy compost.

By autumn the lily stem will have partially rotted under the ground, and bulblets will have developed in the leaf axils towards the bottom of the stem. They can either be left to grow where they are, or removed and treated as already described.

The above method is fairly foolproof. The only problem occurs when the stem rots before it produces bulblets, but luckily this happens only rarely, for example in an abnormally wet summer.

All bulblets generally reach flowering size in two to four years.

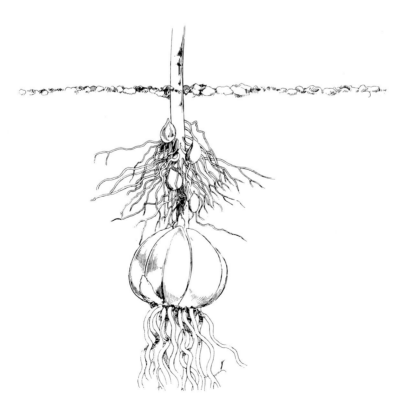

Bulblets can be produced on the underground part of the stem, above the parent bulb. They can be removed and potted up, to be grown on into mature plants

'Enchantment' is a reliable and popular lily which will light up a dark border and produce a cheering effect on even the dullest day (see also page 100)

SCALES

It is possible to produce a new lily plant from a scale removed from the bulb – indeed, this is one of the most widely used methods of propagation. It is extremely important to select only healthy plants that show no signs of disease. Propagation using scales affords no protection against the transfer of virus or other diseases.

The scales should be removed by bending them outwards until they snap off at the base. Either a complete bulb can be 'dismantled' and all the scales used, or a few of the outer scales can be removed and the now smaller parent bulb replanted. It is not necessary to dig up a bulb to remove the scales. It is possible carefully to dig the soil away until the bulb is partly exposed, when some outer scales can be detached, the wounds dusted with a fungicide such as quintozene or carbendazin, and the soil then replaced.

The easiest way to persuade the scales to produce baby bulbs is to put them into a thin polythene bag with some coarse-grade, moist (not wet) vermiculite, which is an expanded micaceous mineral, very light in weight and capable of absorbing large amounts of water. The bag should be very tightly closed, and left in a warm place at about 21 °C (70 °F) – an airing cupboard is ideal. At this stage light is not necessary. Bulblets will form at the point where the scales were detached from the parent bulb. Usually between two and five bulblets form on each scale. The time taken for bulblet formation varies from 4 to 14 weeks, depending on the species or hybrid being used.

The main problem associated with this method of producing plants from scales is that of fungal attack. The conditions of temperature and moisture inside the polythene bag are ideal for fungal growth. It is therefore a wise precaution to dust the scales with a fungicidal powder such as quintozene before they are sealed into the bag.

When the bulblets start to produce roots they should be removed from the bag and planted just under the soil surface with the tips protruding, in boxes or pots of a well-drained potting compost to which leafmould has been added. A layer of grit should then cover the scales. The compost must not be allowed to dry out, but should be kept at about 21°C (70°F) in a place with plenty of light, and leaves should appear fairly quickly.

Scales detached in mid summer should be ready for planting by the autumn, but if they are taken in the autumn they are best left in the polythene bag during the winter and planted in the spring. The new plantlets of lilies that are completely hardy can be hardened off and grown on out of doors, but those of less hardy lilies must have greenhouse protection.

When the new bulblets have formed and the scales are ready for planting, some growers put the bags containing the scales into a cold environment of 0–4°C (32–40°F). They remain there until the spring, when they are planted out in the normal way. Some lilies certainly appear to benefit from this cool treatment, for example hybrids involving *L. auratum* and *L. speciosum*.

Flowers will usually be produced three to six years after the scales are removed and planted, depending on the species or hybrid.

Lilium bulbiferum var. *croceum*, the European orange lily, photographed in the Italian Dolomites. The bulbs are long-lived (see also page 76)

One of the most widely used methods of propagation is from scales: **1.** The bulb is carefully dug up; **2.** Some scales are removed; **3.** These are placed in a polythene bag containing damp vermiculite; **4.** Seal the bag; **5.** In time, bulblets form at the scale bases; **6.** When roots, and sometimes leaves, are produced the scales should be removed from the bag; **7.** Pot these up carefully

CONSERVATION

A plant that is beautiful is always in danger of being dug up for planting in a garden, and lilies are no exception. The threat to a common species is fairly minimal; the risk increases with the rarity of the plant. Lilies have been regarded as desirable garden plants for many years, and some species are now endangered in the wild because of over-collection. In recent years, ease of travel to foreign countries has put pressure on many plants, which attract the attention of the holidaymaker with his ever-ready trowel!

The temptation to dig up lily bulbs (or indeed any other plants) must be resisted. In many countries lilies are protected by law, and offenders are liable to prosecution. The only legitimate way of importing lily species is by seed, and even then you should not be greedy but leave some of the seed to germinate in the wild. A far better way to enjoy lilies is to obtain seed by joining one of the specialist lily societies (see p. 121) that issue an annual seed list to their members. Thus you can have and grow the lilies in your garden without the danger of adding to the ever-increasing list of species that are threatened in the wild. A world without lilies would be a sad world indeed.

6
Pests and Diseases

Gardeners have traditionally considered lilies to be especially prone to attack by marauding armies of pests and fatal infections. It is certainly true that lilies have an ample share of these troubles, but with a little care (including keeping a constant eye open for warning signs) and the help of modern chemicals, there is no reason for one's lilies to turn into hospital patients. Of course, some species and hybrids are more susceptible than others: *L. auratum*, for example, is especially prone to virus attack, but others, such as *L. pyrenaicum*, are practically trouble-free (see also list of Easy Lilies for Beginners on page 115).

GARDEN CHEMICALS

All pesticides and fungicides come with clear instructions for use, and these must be followed absolutely. Do not make the mistake of thinking that a stronger dose of a chemical will kill the pest or disease more quickly or effectively. Not only is it a waste of money to use an excess amount of the product, but the plant may well be damaged as a result.

Opposite: 'Grand Commander' is one of the many cultivars of *Lilium speciosum*, a Far Eastern species which makes a wonderful splash of colour and is easily obtainable from specialist nurseries and garden centres (see also page 92)

Left: 'Black Beauty' is easy to grow and provides a spectacular display of bloom (see also page 97)

Instructions for handling the chemicals must also be heeded. If, for example, the instructions say, 'If spilled on the skin, wash the affected area immediately,' then do so. Many chemicals are very toxic, and irresponsible use can lead to nasty accidents or even disaster.

It is recommended that plants should be sprayed on a dull day or in the evening, as some chemicals tend to damage plant tissue if applied in bright sunshine. An insecticidal spray used late in the day will also be less likely to affect beneficial insects such as bees, which by that time should have returned home.

Finally, always store garden chemicals in properly labelled containers, in a place out of reach of children or pets.

The garden chemicals referred to in this chapter and elsewhere in the book are the active ingredients, not the trade names. A visit to a garden centre or horticultural supplier will reveal that these chemicals are marketed under different trade names by different manufacturers. The active ingredient is always stated (usually in small print) on the label – if you are in any doubt, ask for advice.

PESTS

Aphids

These insects (greenfly are the ones most commonly seen) affect stored bulbs and the stems, leaves and flowers of growing plants. They can also cause indirect trouble by transmitting viruses.

Control is by regular spraying with an insecticide containing dimethoate, gamma-HCH, malathion or diazinon. Products derived from natural sources such as derris or pyrethrum can also be tried.

Slugs

They will attack all parts of the plant and can inflict serious damage at all stages of growth; seedlings are especially at risk. They can be controlled by watering the ground with liquid metaldehyde and by the use of slug pellets. Metaldehyde unfortunately kills not only slugs but other inhabitants of the soil such as the beneficial earthworm. The effects do not stop there, for if slugs that have been poisoned by metaldehyde are eaten by a bird, the bird can also be poisoned. Hedgehogs will also eat poisoned slugs but rarely suffer harm.

It is important that debris such as fallen leaves or weeds, where slugs can lurk, is removed. Aluminium sulphate will kill the eggs of slugs if it is watered on to the soil. It is not inactivated by moderate rain and does not affect other forms of wildlife. An alternative method of preventing slug attack is to put sharp sand below and around the bulb when it is planted. Slugs do not like moving over or through sand or grit.

It has been found that digging the soil thoroughly and leaving it exposed to the elements over the winter will kill off most of the slugs. Drenching the soil with dazomet will finish off any creatures that have escaped the effects of the weather. However, this method can only be used before an area is planted, for example in a new garden or in one that is being drastically renovated.

Lily beetle (Lilioceris lilii)

This is a beetle that has been a pest in most of Europe, particularly southern

England, for years, and appears to be on the increase. It seems to be moving northwards, but is not yet a problem in North America. Both the larvae and the beetles attack lily flowers and leaves. The larvae are about 1 cm ($\frac{2}{5}$ in) long when fully grown, greyish yellow with a dark head, hump-backed and covered with a slimy excrement – not a pretty sight! They are sometimes mistaken for bird droppings. The beetles are bright red with a black head and legs, and grow to about 8 mm ($\frac{1}{3}$ in). The adult beetles spend the winter buried in the soil, and begin to emerge in early spring. Both larvae and beetles can be picked off the plants by hand and destroyed, or a contact insecticide can be used.

Lily bulb thrips
These have pinkish larvae; the adults are black. They attack both stored and growing bulbs, and are found especially at the bases of the bulb scales, where they feed. This weakens the bulbs, which eventually distintegrate. All newly acquired bulbs should be inspected, and if thrips are found the bulbs should be given hot water treatment by immersing them for an hour at 44°C (111°F), or be dusted with gamma-HCH or sprayed with malathion.

Leatherjackets and wireworms
The leatherjacket is the larva of the daddy-long-legs or crane-fly, and may be troublesome in new gardens and near turf. Wireworms are the larvae of click beetles and burrow into the bulbs; they are most common in ground that is newly cultivated. Gamma-HCH dust will control both.

Bulb mites
The adult mites are cream or pinkish, about 1 mm (0.04 in) long, and tend to congregate at the bases of the bulb scales. Badly affected bulbs should be destroyed; a lesser attack can be given the hot water treatment (see thrips above).

Mammals
Deer and rabbits can be a nuisance because they munch the young shoots; a deer fence or one that is rabbitproof is the only complete control. Mice can damage bulbs both in the ground and in store. Traps or poison may work indoors, but outside control is not easy – keeping an underfed cat may help! Some gardeners recommend burying holly leaves or twigs of gorse or other spiny shrubs around the bulbs, or the bulbs can be surrounded (either individually or as a group) by buried chicken wire.

FUNGAL DISEASES

Botrytis
This fungal disease was previously known as 'lily disease', and first manifests itself as dark green spots on the leaves. The spots quickly turn brown and then white, and the leaves begin to die. The disease can rapidly spread up the stem, killing the flower buds or spoiling the flowers. Affected leaves and flowers should be removed and burned, as should any fallen leaves, and the plants should be sprayed with a fungicide that contains benomyl, captan or iprodione.

The fungus enjoys moist conditions and so is encouraged by a wet spring. A preventive spray of Bordeaux Mixture or other copper fungicide, before the fungus strikes, is a good idea, making sure that the surrounding soil (where fungus spores may be lying) is drenched. The spray should be repeated at least twice, at intervals of two weeks.

Note that in spring the young leaves can be affected by frost, which gives the appearance of botrytis damage.

Basal rot

A disease caused by the fungus *Fusarium oxysporum* that affects the bases of the bulb scales, quickly causing complete disintegration. The fungus lives on plant debris in the soil and can remain there for some years, so if the disease is discovered, lilies should not be planted in the same place unless the soil is sterilized (a 2 per cent formalin solution is suitable). Basal rot generally comes into the garden by means of infected bulbs, and newly acquired bulbs should be examined carefully. Badly affected bulbs should be burned, slightly affected ones may have the rotted parts removed and should then be immersed in 0.5 per cent benomyl for an hour.

Species and hybrids vary considerably in their susceptibility to basal rot.

Opposite: *Lilium tsingtauense* in a semi-shady part of the garden where the orange flowers brighten the surrounding ferns (see also page 92)

Right: 'Sterling Star' is a most attractive white-flowered cultivar (see page 112), here growing through *Helichrysum petiolare* to produce a beautiful cool effect

Rhizoctonia

A soil-borne fungus that lives on dead and dying plant material. It occurs most often on well-drained and sandy soils. It shows if, in the summer, the plant turns yellow and often wilts, and when dug up the bulb will be seen to have dead or dying roots and may have rotted at the base. Really rotted bulbs will have to be destroyed, but if the damage is not too extensive the bulb can be cleaned up and treated with a fungicide such as quintozene or carbendazin.

Blue mould

This disease is caused by the fungus *Penicillium cyclopium*, which attacks the bulbs. It shows as small, brown depressed spots on the bulb scales that gradually grow larger and develop a white fungal growth in the centre; when spores are produced the colour changes to blue-green. In the early stages of the disease infected scales should be removed and burned, but badly affected bulbs must be destroyed.

VIRUS DISEASES

Viruses that affect lilies are spread by aphids, so control of these insects is important. No cure has yet been found and affected bulbs should be destroyed before the virus can infect more plants. Viruses can also be spread by handling infected bulbs, so after touching such plants, hands must be thoroughly washed. On the positive side, viruses are not known to affect the seeds.

Lily mottle virus   healthy   virus infected

Lily mosaic

This serious disease is widespread; it is caused by lily mottle virus or cucumber mosaic virus. It is spread by aphids, and usually produces streaking or mottling of the leaves followed by distortion. Affected plants produce fewer flowers than normal, and these may display broken colour or be deformed, or the buds may fail to open properly. *L. speciosum* and *L. auratum* are especially vulnerable to infection.

Lily mottle virus

This virus is responsible for 'breaking' in the flowers of tulips: the normal flower colour is variegated and streaked with another colour. Rembrandt tulips, whose main feature is their broken flowers, should never be grown near lilies in case the virus is transferred.

Lily rosette or yellowflat

A virus disease that produces dwarfed plants with congested, curled, pale green or yellowish leaves. If flowers are produced at all they tend not to develop beyond the bud stage. The virus affects the bulbs, which become smaller than normal and flattened, and tend to split up. *L. longiflorum* is especially susceptible.

Other troubles

The effect of **frost damage** can look similar to infection by virus. *L. regale* is especially prone to damage and should be grown in a sheltered place. Exposure to cold wind can cause the leaves of lilies to turn purplish.

Purplish leaves can also be produced by **inadequate soil drainage**; in this case the leaves eventually turn brown and shrivel. Lilies are sensitive to poorly drained conditions, which usually result in root rot. Affected bulbs should be dug up, the rotted roots removed and the bulbs replanted in a more suitable place.

If the leaves turn yellow between the veins, **chlorosis** is probably the cause. It occurs most commonly in acid-loving species when they are grown in an alkaline soil. In such circumstances chelated iron should be watered on to the soil, which should also be made less alkaline by the incorporation of peat or leafmould.

Fasciation is usually caused by an injury to the young growing point of the plant. The stem flattens and often becomes considerably misshapen, and the leaves are rather small. Fasciation usually affects the plant only for the year in which it occurs; in the absence of further injury, growth will be normal in the following year.

A lily showing fasciation

A to Z of
Lilies

'Journey's End' is a brilliant cultivar which should be tried in any
garden in need of brightening up (see also page 105)

Naming Lilies

There are just over a hundred species in the genus *Lilium*, and of these about ninety are in cultivation, though some are difficult to grow and are only in the collections of a few specialists.

On the whole, the species and hybrids described on the following pages are all available either from nurseries or through the seed lists of specialist societies. In addition, a small number of rare or difficult lilies have been included here because of their beauty or interest.

Over the years, breeders have produced a huge number of hybrids or cultivars. A glance through the catalogues of bulb dealers will quickly reveal that the number of hybrids well exceeds the number of species offered – in fact some catalogues do not list any species at all. Serious production of hybrids began in the last quarter of the 19th century, and after 1900 the number of cultivars and strains began to increase. However, the vast majority of hybrids that we now grow in our gardens were produced after 1940, and lily-breeding shows no decline in the 1980s. Lily-breeders have been and are active in Britain, Holland, Germany, the USA and Canada, New Zealand, Australia, Japan and South Africa, all countries where lilies grow well, and where they have been cultivated for some time. Modern techniques such as tissue culture are now helping to clean up lily stocks and produce virus-free plants.

The *International Lily Register* lists about 3500 names, though not all of these are still in existence – as with any group of plants, cultivars are produced and some die out when they are superseded by cultivars that are better in some way.

In lilies, the term 'hybrid' applies to two categories, the grex or strain, and the clone. These are explained by the following example (the names used are invented). When two different lilies are crossed, the resultant seedlings will normally exhibit a certain amount of variation. This original range of seedlings, should it prove to be promising commercially or otherwise, is given a name, e.g. Kew Wonder. All the seedlings from the cross will bear this name and all are members of the named grex or strain.

The lily-breeder may wish to grow on the Kew Wonder grex, and will probably destroy those plants that are inferior in some way, perhaps less vigorous or not conforming to the required colour. Eventually, particular plants can be selected and given clonal names, e.g. 'Red Pagoda' with ruby red flowers or 'Hooker's Pride' with exceptionally tall stems. A clone must be propagated vegetatively to preserve its distinguishing features.

Grex or strain names are written or printed in ordinary roman type; the names of clones, also roman, are enclosed in single quotation marks. Thus *Lilium* Kew Wonder is a grex, *Lilium* 'Red Pagoda' is a clone.

Since 1958 registration of lily grex and clone names has been undertaken by the Royal Horticultural Society, which is the International Registration Authority for the genus and maintains a register of names. The 3rd edition of the *Register* was published in 1982, and supplements have been issued that list subsequent registrations.

The reader may wonder why it is necessary to have a register of lily names.

THE CLASSIFICATION OF LILY CULTIVARS INTO DIVISIONS

I Hybrids derived from such species or hybrid groups as *L. lancifolium*, *L. cernuum*, *L. davidii*, *L. leichtlinii*, *L. maculatum*, *L. × hollandicum*, *L. amabile*, *L. concolor* and *L. bulbiferum*.

I(a) Early flowering lilies with upright flowers, single or in an umbel.

I(b) Those with outward-facing flowers.

I(c) Those with pendent flowers.

II Hybrids of martagon type of which one parent has been a form of *L. martagon* or *L. hansonii*.

III Hybrids derived from *L. candidum*, *L. chalcedonicum* and other related European species (but excluding *L. martagon*).

IV Hybrids of American species.

V Hybrids derived from *L. longiflorum* and *L. formosanum*.

VI Hybrid Trumpet Lilies and Aurelian Hybrids derived from Asiatic species including *L. henryi*, but excluding those derived from *L. auratum*, *L. speciosum*, *L. japonicum* and *L. rubellum*.

VI(a) Those with trumpet-shaped flowers.

VI(b) Those with bowl-shaped and outward-facing flowers.

VI(c) Those with pendent flowers.

VI(d) Those with flat, star-shaped flowers.

VII Hybrids of Far Eastern species such as *L. auratum*, *L. speciosum*, *L. japonicum* and *L. rubellum*, including any of their hybrids with *L. henryi*.

VII(a) Those with trumpet-shaped flowers.

VII(b) Those with bowl-shaped flowers.

VII(c) Those with flat flowers.

VII(d) Those with recurved flowers.

With breeders all over the world producing and naming cultivars, it is very likely that they will choose the same names. An example that actually occurred is that of the clone 'Tangerine'. Some forty years ago Jan de Graaff of Oregon selected a lightly spotted tangerine-orange lily from his own Rainbow Hybrids (which were produced from a cross between *L. lancifolium* and *L. × hollandicum*), and named it 'Tangerine'. At the same time, the firm of W. A. Constable Ltd selected a yellow lily with chocolate-brown spots from a cross between *L. davidii* var. *willmottiae* and a selection from *L. maculatum* called 'Mahogany'; it was also christened 'Tangerine'.

The gardener who orders 'Tangerine' cannot, therefore, be certain which clone he will receive. To avoid confusion it is most important that names are not duplicated. Even when a cultivar dies out completely its name may not be reused. It is also important that all breeders submit their chosen names to the Registrar so that he can check that the name has not already been used. If the name has been used, the breeder will have to think of an alternative.

The scheme set out below shows the horticultural classification of lily cultivars into divisions, as now used in the *International Lily Register*. In the A to Z of lily cultivars (see p. 95 ff.) the division is given after the name of the cultivar.

Lily Species

Lily seeds have two types of germination, known as epigeal and hypogeal, and in either case germination can be immediate or delayed. For more information on this subject refer back to page 51.

L. amabile This species has five to ten nodding, turk's-cap flowers which smell rather unpleasant and are red spotted with black. The stem is 30–90 cm (1–3 ft) tall, downy, leafless in the lower part. Stem-rooting. The leaves are scattered and narrow. Germination – immediate epigeal. Flowering time – early to mid summer.

Native to Korea, this hardy lily will grow in acid or alkaline soil, and likes a position in sun or semi-shade. It is small enough to be grown at the back of a rock garden or raised bed.

Var. *luteum* has yellow flowers and tends to be less vigorous, at least in some places.

L. auratum (golden-rayed lily) A truly magnificent lily native to Japan. The very fragrant bowl-shaped flowers face outwards, and there are usually one to six, but sometimes as many as 30, each segment white with a yellow central band, and generally spotted with crimson or yellow. It is stem-rooting and the stem grows 60–150 cm (2–5 ft), sometimes more. The narrow leaves are scattered, and each has a short stalk. Germination – delayed hypogeal. Flowering time – late summer to early autumn.

This beautiful lily, whose flowers can be as much as 30 cm (12 in) across, grows best in an acid or neutral soil with plenty of

Opposite: *Lilium amabile* var. *luteum* comes from Korea. The flowers smell rather nasty, but the cheerful colour compensates for this disadvantage

Right: *Lilium auratum* var. *platyphyllum*

leafmould; it will not thrive in a limy soil. It should not be planted in full sun, and is ideal for planting among shrubs. In tubs it can look most impressive. It lasts well as a cut flower.

L. auratum is especially affected by virus disease; if possible, bulbs should be bought from nurseries offering virus-free stock.
Var. *platyphyllum* has broader leaves and flowers with fewer spots. 'Crimson Beauty' is a lovely cultivar that has a band of cherry-red up the centre of each segment.

L. bolanderi The three to eight or some-times up to 18 flowers are outward-facing to nodding, funnel-shaped, scented, each segment deep crimson, spotted with darker red or purple and yellowish to-wards the base. The stems reach 40–90 cm ($1\frac{1}{2}$–3 ft) in height, and the narrow, grey-green leaves are borne in whorls. Not stem-rooting. Germination – delayed hypogeal. Flowering time – mid summer.

This species is native to the western USA (Oregon and California) and is not com-mon in cultivation. It tends to be rather short-lived, so must be raised from seed frequently to keep a stock of plants. It will tolerate alkaline soils, but does best in a peaty or humus-rich soil, in full sun. It is one of the few lilies with grey-green leaves.

L. bulbiferum (orange lily) This is the only European species with upward-facing flowers. It is found in mountainous areas in south-west and central Europe. It has one to five, or sometimes more, upward-facing, cup-shaped flowers. The segments are orange-red spotted with maroon or blackish, and have warts towards the clawed base. It is stem-rooting and the stem is 40–150 cm ($1\frac{1}{2}$–5 ft) tall. The scat-tered leaves are narrow with a ciliate margin and have bulbils in the axils. Germination – delayed hypogeal. Flowering time – early to mid summer.

This species will grow in any well-drained soil, in sun or semi-shade. The bulbs are long-lived.
Var. *croceum* (*L. croceum*) is more com-monly seen in gardens than *L. bulbiferum*

itself. It has orange rather than orange-red flowers and lacks bulbils in the leaf axils.
Hybrids
L. × *hollandicum* is the name given to a group of hybrids between *L. bulbiferum* and *L. maculatum*. They have upward-facing, cup-shaped flowers, which can be red, orange or yellow. Height is about 70 cm (2 ft 4 in) or more. They are especially useful as cut flowers. They are often listed erroneously in catalogues as *L.* × *umbellatum*.

L. callosum A pretty lily that is not at all common in gardens, possibly because the bulbs are short-lived and it is necessary repeatedly to raise seedlings. The scattered leaves are very narrow, and there are usually three to five pendent Turk's-cap flowers. The segments are orange-red, faintly dotted with black towards the base. It has stem roots, and the stems grow to 90 cm (3 ft). Germination – immediate epigeal. Flowering time – late summer.

This species is from the Far East. It is tolerant of limy soils, and likes plenty of humus in the soil and a sunny position.

L. canadense (Canada lily, meadow lily) A species from eastern North America, with up to 30 funnel-shaped, nodding flowers. The segments are yellow, usually spotted with maroon or purplish brown towards the base, and with recurved tips. The bulb is stoloniferous and there are a few stem roots on the stem, which grows to about 1.5 m (5 ft). The narrow leaves are mostly borne in whorls, though there are a few scattered at the top of the stem. Germina-tion – delayed hypogeal. Flowering time – mid to late summer.

This species dislikes limy soil and dry conditions. In the wild it grows in places that are wettish but not stagnant. It will thrive in sun or semi-shade, and looks lovely growing among acid-loving shrubs such as pieris or rhododendrons.
Var. *coccineum* has red flowers, yellow in the throat.
Var. *editorum* has red flowers with rather narrow segments, and leaves that are broader than those of *L. canadense* itself.

L. candidum (Madonna lily) Native to south-east Europe and the Near East. Stem roots are lacking; the red-purple stem grows 90–200 cm (3–6 ft), with very narrow, scattered leaves. The 5 to 20 white, funnel-shaped flowers face outwards, and are very fragrant. Each segment is yellow at the base and slightly recurved at the tip. Germination – immediate epigeal. Flowering time – mid summer.

L. candidum differs from most other species in producing basal leaves that last throughout the winter. It grows best in full sun in neutral or limy soil, and should be planted shallowly in early autumn, with the tip of the bulb more or less showing. It mixes well with other plants and is often grown in the herbaceous border.

Hybrids

The earliest hybrid between European species is L. × testaceum (the Nankeen lily) which was produced in cultivation in Germany or Holland in about 1810. The parents are L. candidum and L. chalcedonicum, and like its parents it will grow on limy soil. The 6 to 12 very fragrant, nodding flowers are tawny yellow to pale orange, in shape somewhat between a funnel and turk's-cap, and usually have some reddish spots inside. The red anthers have orange pollen, which contrasts beautifully with the segments. The 1–1.5 m (3–5 ft) stems are purplish and bear very narrow, scattered leaves. Early to mid summer. Like those of L. candidum, the bulbs should be planted in early autumn, in a sunny place.

L. catesbaei A species from the south-eastern USA with one or sometimes two widely cup-shaped, upward-facing flowers. Each segment is deep yellow, turning scarlet towards the sharply pointed, recurved tip, and spotted with maroon towards the long-clawed base. Stem roots lacking. The stem is 30–60 cm (1–2 ft) tall, and the scattered leaves are narrow and adpressed to the stem. Germination – immediate epigeal. Flowering time – mid summer to mid autumn.

This is a very rare species, which is difficult to cultivate but is included because of its unusual and attractive flowers, in which the claw of each segment is half the length of the whole segment. It is only just frost-hardy, and needs glass protection in colder areas.

L. cernuum This lily is found from Korea north to the north-eastern USSR. It has up to six or more powerfully scented turk's-cap flowers, which are drooping, pinkish purple or sometimes white, with purple spots. There are stem roots, and the stem grows 30–60 cm (1–2 ft) tall with very narrow, scattered leaves. Germination – immediate epigeal. Flowering time – early to mid summer.

The bulb is rather short-lived so this species must be propagated frequently to maintain the stock. It is tolerant of lime, but does best in a peaty soil. It is a suitable species for the rock garden. Not an easy lily, but one that is well worth persevering with.

L. chalcedonicum *(L. heldreichii)* This lily has up to 12 turk's-cap flowers, which are pendent and have a smell some people find unpleasant. Each segment is red or orange-red and has warts towards the base. Stem roots present. The stem grows 45–150 cm (1½–5 ft), and bears narrow, scattered leaves with a ciliate margin that looks silvery. The lower leaves are spreading, and the upper ones are adpressed to the stem. Germination – delayed epigeal. Flowering time – mid to late summer.

This lily, which comes from Greece and Albania, is rather susceptible to fungal diseases, and it is a good idea to raise seedlings from time to time. It will grow in any well-drained soil and likes a position in full sun or semi-shade. It is a fine species for the herbaceous border.
Var. **maculatum** has flowers with deep purple or maroon spots and streaks, tends to be more vigorous, and flowers a little earlier.

L. ciliatum A rare lily from north-east Turkey, well worth growing, despite its not very nice smell, if it can be obtained. The turk's-cap flowers are pendent, and

Lilium chalcedonicum
(see page 77)

upward-facing, fragrant flowers, which have orange-red segments, slightly recurved at the tips. Germination – immediate epigeal. Flowering time – early to mid summer. A disadvantage of this lily is that the bulbs are not long-lived. It will grow in any well-drained soil, in either full sun or dappled shade. Its height makes it a suitable species for the rock garden.

Var. **pulchellum** has a green stem and spotted flowers, and flower buds that are hairy.

L. dauricum This species usually has one to six, sometimes more, open cup-shaped flowers that face upwards. Each segment is red to orange-red, yellow towards the clawed base, usually spotted with brownish red or purple, and with warts, the tip slightly recurved. The bulb is stoloniform and there are stem roots. The stem reaches 75 cm ($2\frac{1}{2}$ ft) and has white cobwebby hairs towards the top. It bears narrow scattered leaves, which often have cobwebby hairs on the margins. Germination – immediate epigeal. Flowering time – early to mid summer. In favourable conditions flowers can be produced two years after the seed is sown.

there are usually five to eight, though vigorous plants can produce up to 20. Each segment is cream or pale yellow, with purple-brown streaks towards the base and woolly hairs at the tip. The pollen is orange. It is stem-rooting and the stem grows 60–160 cm ($2–5\frac{1}{2}$ ft). The narrow, scattered leaves have ciliate margins. Germination – delayed hypogeal. Flowering time – early to mid summer. It grows best in semi-shade in a neutral or acid soil.

L. columbianum This species grows along the Pacific coast of North America, from southern Canada to California. There are six to ten, but occasionally many more, nodding, turk's-cap flowers, and each segment is yellow to orange-red, spotted with purple-red towards the base. The bulb is sub-rhizomatous. It lacks stem roots, and the stem attains 2 m (6 ft). The narrow leaves are mainly whorled, with the upper ones scattered. Germination – delayed hypogeal. Flowering time – mid summer. This is an easy lily that grows best in semi-shade on acid soil, and looks good planted among shrubs.

L. concolor A pretty Far Eastern species that is stem-rooting and has purplish stems 30–90 cm (1–3 ft) tall. The scattered leaves are very narrow, with slightly ciliate margins. There are up to ten star-shaped,

Lilium concolor var.
pulchellum

which are borne two or three to a pedicel. Var. **unicolor** has shorter stems, less than 1 m (3 ft), very crowded leaves and fewer, paler flowers, which either lack spots or have spots that are reddish or mauve. Var. **willmottiae** has stems growing 2 m (6 ft) that tend to bend under the weight of the flowers, of which there can be as many as 40.

L. duchartrei This species usually has six, sometimes up to 12 fragrant, nodding, turk's-cap flowers, which are white, often purple-flushed and with purple spots and streaks. The bulb is stoloniform. Stem-rooting. The stem is 60–100 cm (2–3 ft) tall and bears narrow scattered leaves. Germination – immediate epigeal. Flowering time – mid summer. It is tolerant of limy soil that should not be allowed to dry out in the growing season – thus it tends to grow better in northern areas. It is a native of south-west China.

Lilium hansonii (see page 80)

Lilium humboldtii (see page 80)

This easy-to-grow lily has no real soil preference, though it seems to thrive best in a soil without lime. It will grow in full sun or light shade. It is native to north-east Asia.
Var. **alpinum** grows only 10–12 cm (4–$4\frac{3}{4}$ in) tall.

L. davidii This lily comes from south-west China and has a bulb that is sometimes stoloniform. It is stem-rooting, and the stem grows 1–1.5 m (3–5 ft) in height. The very narrow, scattered leaves usually have cobwebby hairs in the axils. The buds are often hairy, and open to produce 5 to 20 pendent turk's-cap flowers. The red or orange-red segments are warty in the lower part and covered with dense, deep purple raised spots, except at the tips. Germination – immediate epigeal. Flowering time – mid to late summer.

This species likes a humus-rich soil, where it will produce plentiful bulblets. It is lime-tolerant, although happier in a neutral or acid soil. It likes a position in sun or light shade and can withstand limited dry conditions. It is a useful species for the herbaceous border.
Var. **macranthum** has taller stems to 2 m (6 ft), and larger, bright orange flowers

L. formosanum A beautiful stem-rooting lily from Taiwan. Stem 30–150 cm (1–5 ft) tall, with very narrow scattered leaves. Flowers one or two, fragrant, trumpet-shaped, outward-facing, white, usually flushed with reddish purple outside, the segments recurved at the tips. Germination – immediate epigeal. Flowering time – late summer to early autumn.

In good conditions this lily can bear flowers 6–12 months after the seed is sown. It should have a place in full sun and is a fine tub plant. It is not reliably hardy, and in colder areas is better grown under glass. It is rather prone to virus disease, and new plants should be raised from seed from time to time. It is useful for cutting.

Var. **pricei** has a shorter stem, usually less than 60 cm (2 ft), and solitary flowers more deeply flushed with reddish purple. It flowers a little earlier and is slightly more hardy. Sited with care, it makes a beautiful addition to the rock garden.

L. grayi This lily has up to 12 scented, bell-shaped flowers, deep red outside, paler inside and often yellow inside at the base, with purple spots. The bulb is stoloniferous; stem roots are absent. The stem is up to 1.75 m (5½ ft) in height, with whorls of narrow leaves. Germination – delayed hypogeal. Flowering time – mid summer. This species likes an acid soil with plenty of moisture while it is growing, in either a sunny or slightly shady position. It comes from the eastern USA. An uncommon lily, both in the wild and in gardens.

L. hansonii The 3 to 12 nodding turk's-cap flowers are very fragrant, and have very thick orange-yellow segments with purplish brown spots towards the base. An eastern Asiatic species, with stem roots. The stem grows 1–1.5 m (3–5 ft) tall, and bears narrow leaves mostly in whorls. Germination – delayed hypogeal. Flowering time – early to mid summer. The long-lived bulbs are hardy and will grow in any soil, but should not be planted in deep shade; it is ideal for glades in a woodland garden. An easily grown lily with long-lasting flowers.

L. henrici This species has up to seven somewhat nodding, broadly bell-shaped flowers. The segments are whitish, pink-flushed on the back; the inner segments are dark purple at the base. Stem 90–120 cm (3–4 ft) tall, with very narrow scattered leaves. Germination – immediate epigeal. Flowering time – mid summer. A lily from western China which thrives in an acid soil with plenty of humus; it appreciates light shade. It grows better in northern areas than southern, probably because it dislikes dry soil conditions.

L. henryi A lily with 4 to 20, or sometimes more, nodding, scented, turk's-cap flowers, with one or two on each pedicel. Each orange segment has dark spots and prominent warts towards the base. Stem roots are present, and the arching stems are 1–3 m (3–10 ft) tall. The narrow leaves are scattered, and sometimes have bulbils growing in the axils. Germination – immediate epigeal. Flowering time – late summer.

An easy lily, native to central China, which grows well on limy soils and in semi-shade. On acid soils it gradually deteriorates, eventually failing completely. It looks good in a herbaceous border. Planting it among shrubs obviates the need to stake the tall stems.

Var. **citrinum** has pale yellow flowers, lightly spotted with brown or red-brown.

L. humboldtii A lily from California, USA, which usually has 10 to 15 scented, nodding, turk's-cap flowers, occasionally as many as 80, which are yellow to orange with maroon or purple spots towards the centre. The bulb is sub-rhizomatous. Stem roots are lacking; the stem can attain 2.75 m (9 ft). The narrow leaves are borne in whorls. Germination – delayed hypogeal. Flowering time – mid summer.

This species must have especially good drainage (after flowering the bulbs should be kept almost dry until early winter) and can be planted in sun or light shade.

Var. **ocellatum** differs in having stem roots and segments which are red at the tips; the spots are encircled with crimson.

L. iridollae This species has one to eight pendent turk's-cap flowers, which are yellow with brown spots. The bulb is stoloniferous. Stem roots are present, and the stem grows to 1.75 m (5½ ft). Most of the narrow leaves are borne in whorls. Germination – immediate hypogeal. Flowering time – mid to late summer. A rare species from the south-eastern USA, which is also rare in gardens. This species produces a tuft of basal leaves in the autumn that remains throughout the winter.

L. japonicum The one to five fragrant, broadly funnel-shaped flowers are outward-facing, pink, with each segment recurved at the tip. Stem-rooting. Stem 45–100 cm (1½–3 ft) tall with rather few, narrow, scattered leaves that have short stalks. Germination – delayed hypogeal. Flowering time – mid summer.

This Japanese species is not an easy one to grow, but it is beautiful. The soil, preferably acid or neutral, should not be allowed to dry out, and the bulbs should be planted in semi-shade.

L. kelleyanum (*L. nevadense, L. shastense*) A native of the western USA (California and Oregon) that has up to 25 turk's-cap flowers, which are scented and pendent. Each segment varies from greeny yellow to yellow or orange, and has purplish red or brown spots towards the base. It has a rhizomatous bulb and lacks stem roots. The stems grow to 1 m (3 ft), sometimes more. The narrow or oval leaves are scattered, whorled or a mixture of the two. Germination – delayed hypogeal. Flowering time – mid summer.

This species likes an acid soil rich in humus, and a position in sun or light shade. It prefers the bulb to be in damp soil but the aerial parts to be dry and warm; a sunny stream-side is therefore ideal, but not something every gardener possesses!

L. kelloggii A species with up to 20 very fragrant, nodding turk's-cap flowers, with mauve, pink or white segments, each usually with a yellow band in the lower part and with purple or maroon dots towards the base. Not stem-rooting. Stem 30–125 cm (1–4¼ ft) in height, with most of the narrow leaves in whorls. Germination – delayed hypogeal. Flowering time – mid summer.

A species from western USA (Oregon and California) whose pretty flowers have stamens with unexpected red or orange anthers. It prefers semi-shade; if grown in a sunny place the flower colour fades very quickly.

L. kesselringianum A lily that looks rather like *L. monadelphum* but is much less often seen in gardens. There are one to six strongly scented, nodding turk's-cap flowers, which are cream or pale yellow with reddish or purple spots in the centre. The segments are not strongly recurved. The stem grows 1–1.4 m (3–4½ ft) tall and bears narrow, scattered leaves. Not generally stem-rooting. Germination – delayed hypogeal. Flowering time – mid to late summer. Like *L. monadelphum*, this lily is tolerant of lime and prefers to grow in semi-shade. It comes from north-east Turkey and from Georgia, USSR.

L. lancifolium (*L. tigrinum*) (tiger lily) A popular lily from the Far East. The pendent turk's-cap flowers usually number 12 to 20, though there may be as many as 40. They are pinkish orange to orange-red, with dark purple spots and warts. Stem-rooting. Stem 60–150 cm (2–5 ft) tall or more, the narrow scattered leaves with black-purple bulbils in the axils. Germination – immediate epigeal. Flowering time – late summer to early autumn.

An easy lily, *L. lancifolium* likes a fertile acid soil (though it will grow adequately on lime) and can be grown in sun or semi-shade. It is attractive grown in the herbaceous border, and is useful for planting in pots or tubs, and for cutting.

Most of the cultivated stock of this lily is virus-infected. The virus does not affect the plants visibly to any great extent but aphids can transfer the virus to nearby lilies, therefore aphid control is very important.

Lilium kesselringianum (see page 81)

Var. **flaviflorum** has yellow flowers and is often badly affected by virus disease. 'Yellow Tiger' is a selection from var. *flaviflorum* with yellow, purple-spotted flowers. Var. **fortunei** is a larger plant, with many orange-red flowers on a densely woolly stem.

Var. **splendens** is a vigorous grower with large, bright orange flowers.

Cultivars

'Flore Pleno' is double flowered with 24 to 36 rather narrow segments. It is one of those flowers that people either love or hate.

L. lankongense This lily, which comes from Tibet and south-west China, has a stoloniform bulb and is stem-rooting. The stem attains 1.2 m (4 ft), and bears narrow scattered leaves. There are up to 15 scented,

Lilium leichtlinii var. *maximowiczii*

pendent turk's-cap flowers. Each segment is pink or mauvish with red-purple spots, especially on the margin, and has a central green band. Germination – immediate epigeal. Flowering time – mid summer.

Although it tolerates lime, it grows best in a neutral or acid soil with a lot of humus. It is easier to grow in northern areas, where it enjoys full sun; in southern areas it should be grown in dappled shade. It is rather prone to virus diseases, but this unfortunate feature is not transmitted to its progeny when it is used in hybridizing.

Recent research suggests that this lily should now be included under *L. duchartrei*, because in the wild the distinguishing features of the two species merge, making them hard to separate. The plants we cultivate in our gardens, however, because they come from opposite ends of the species' range, *can* be separated from one another.

L. ledebourii A rather uncommon lily from north-west Iran and Azerbaijan in the USSR. There are up to five fragrant nodding turk's-cap flowers, which are creamy white, turning greenish yellow with age and with red or purple dots in the centre. The anthers are orange-red. Stem-rooting. The stems grow 1–1.2 m (3–4 ft) tall and bear very narrow scattered leaves. Germination – delayed hypogeal. Flowering time – mid summer.

This species is the only lily known to grow in Iran. It is not often seen in gardens, which is a pity because its flowers, which have rather thick, waxy segments, are delightfully scented. It grows best in a soil with plenty of leafmould, in a semi-shady position.

L. leichtlinii A species from the Far East with a rhizomatous bulb. The one to six nodding turk's-cap flowers are yellow, with purplish maroon spots. Stem roots are present, and the stem grows to 1.2 m (4 ft) tall. The very narrow leaves are scattered, and often have white hairs at the axils. Germination – immediate epigeal. Flowering time – early summer to early autumn. It grows best in an acid soil in partial shade.
Var. **_maximowiczii_** has a taller stem, up to 2.5 m (8 ft) in height, and reddish orange flowers spotted with purplish brown; it is generally considered to be easier to grow than the species itself.

L. leucanthum This lily, which comes from western China, is cultivated only as var. _centifolium_. The narrow leaves are scattered, and there are up to 18 scented, outward-facing or slightly nodding funnel-shaped flowers, which are white,

flushed outside with purple-red, and yellow at the base inside. The segments are strongly recurved at the tips. It is stem-rooting and the stem reaches 2–3 m (6–10 ft). Germination – immediate epigeal. Flowering time – mid summer.

This lily tolerates limy soils and will grow in full sun provided the lower part of the plant is shaded, for example by other plants. Non-flowering plants may produce bulbils in the leaf axils.

L. longiflorum (Easter lily, Bermuda lily) This lily is important commercially, being grown in huge numbers for the cut-flower trade in the USA, Japan, Bermuda, South Africa, New Zealand and Holland, to mention only some countries. It comes originally from the Ryukyu Islands, which lie south of Japan, and possibly from Taiwan. The one to six scented, trumpet-to funnel-shaped flowers face outwards or

Lilium longiflorum

Lilium mackliniae
(see page 84)

slightly upwards, and are white with the tips of the segments slightly recurved. It is stem-rooting, and the stem grows 30–100 cm (1–3 ft) tall. The narrow leaves are scattered. Germination – immediate epigeal. Flowering time – mid summer.

This is a lime-tolerant species but a tender one, which in cooler areas is usually grown under glass, when it will flower in late spring. It looks good grown in pots or tubs. It is an easy lily to force, and lovely as a cut flower. It grows very rapidly from seed, often producing flowers within six months.

Cultivars
Many cultivars have been described. 'Albomarginatum' has leaves broadly margined with white. 'Georgia' is very free-flowering and has leaves that are longer than usual. 'Holland's Glory' is one of the hardiest, with up to 12 flowers about 20 cm (8 in) long. 'White Queen' has white trumpets with a green throat.

L. mackliniae This species has one to six more or less nodding, purplish pink, broadly bell-shaped flowers. Stem-rooting, with the stem up to 50 cm (20 in) in height, exceptionally reaching 1 m (3 ft). The narrow leaves are scattered, or in whorls near the top of the stem. Germination – immediate epigeal. Flowering time – early to mid summer.

This beautiful species from north-east India is easy to raise from seed, which is lucky as the plant if often affected by virus disease. It grows best in a neutral or acid soil, in dappled shade, and looks especially beautiful in a woodland or peat garden. It is not happy in dry conditions. In cooler areas the bulbs should always be protected from frost.

L. maculatum (L. wilsonii) The one to several cup-shaped flowers face upwards, and can be yellow, orange or red with dark spots; each segment is clawed at the base. The bulb is stoloniform. It is stem-rooting, with the stem up to 60 cm (2 ft) tall with narrow scattered leaves. Germination – immediate epigeal. Flowering time – early to late summer.

This is a rather variable species that comes from Japan. It is best grown in full sun. Some botanists consider that it may be a hybrid between L. dauricum and L. concolor.
Var. **bukozanense** has orange flowers with narrow segments, borne on a curving stem.
Var. **flavum** has yellow flowers and is sometimes offered under the name L. wilsonii var. flavum.

L. maritimum There are up to 20 nodding, broadly funnel-shaped flowers, which are deep red to reddish orange with maroon spots. Each segment is recurved at the tip. The bulb is rhizomatous. This lily is not stem-rooting; the stem reaches 30–70 cm (1 ft–2 ft 4 in), sometimes up to 2 m (6 ft). The narrow leaves are scattered, though taller plants may have some leaves in whorls. Germination – delayed hypogeal. Flowering time – early to late summer.

This lily, from California, is not often seen in our gardens. It likes a light, humus-rich soil in dappled shade. The bulbs sprout early in the spring and should be protected from frost.

L. martagon (martagon lily) The nodding turk's-cap flowers number up to 50 and are scented, though some people find the scent unpleasant. The segments are white, pink or dark purplish red and often have spots. This lily has the largest range of any species, being native to Europe and to Asia as far east as Mongolia. It is naturalized in some parts of England. It has stem roots, and the stems are 90–200 cm (3–6 ft) tall, usually purplish and sometimes hairy. The narrow to oval leaves are in whorls. Germination – delayed hypogeal. Flowering time – early to mid summer. It is an easy, long-lived plant for acid or alkaline soils in sun or semi-shade. It is a marvellous plant for a garden with open woodland.

L. martagon has been divided into a number of varieties; the following are recommended.
Var. **album** has green, hairless stems and white unspotted flowers; it is ideal for

brightening up the foliage of shrubs that have finished flowering, which can often be dull.

Var. **cattaniae** (var. *dalmaticum*) has dark maroon, unspotted flowers, which open from hairy buds.

Var. **caucasicum** has lilac-pink flowers with dark red spots, which open from downy buds.

Hybrids

L. × *dalhansonii* is a hybrid between *L. martagon* var. *cattaniae* and *L. hansonii*. This plant bears many maroon flowers, heavily spotted and flushed with orange at the centre of each segment. Height 1–1.5 m (3– 5 ft). Early summer. The name *L.* × *dalhansonii* covers all the *L. martagon/ hansonii* hybrids, from which several clones have been selected and named, e.g. 'Marhan', 'Mrs R.O. Backhouse', and 'St Nicholas' which is now extremely rare.

L. michauxii (Carolina lily) The flowers of this lily are turk's-cap, nodding and scented. There are usually one or two, sometimes up to five. They are orange-red to pale crimson with black or purple spots, and yellowish in the throat. The bulb is stoloniferous. It is stem-rooting, with the stem up to 1.2 m (4 ft) tall. The leaves are narrowly oval, mostly in whorls. Germination – delayed hypogeal. Flowering time – mid to late summer.

This lily from the south-eastern USA, although not difficult to grow, is not common in gardens, possibly because it is necessary to protect the bulbs well in winter in case they are killed by frost. It likes a light, acid soil and full sun.

L. michiganense A species from eastern North America, rather similar to *L. canadense*. It has nodding turk's-cap flowers, usually three to six but sometimes up to 25; they are orange to red with deep red or purple spots. The bulb is stoloniferous. Stem roots are absent; the stem is 60–150 cm (2–5 ft) tall, occasionally more. The leaves are narrow to narrowly oval, in whorls. Germination – delayed hypogeal. Flowering time – early to mid summer. It thrives in dampish but not stagnant conditions, and likes a sunny position.

L. monadelphum (*L. szovitsianum*) The flowers are between funnel-shaped and turk's-cap. There are usually one to five, but sometimes as many as 30; they are nodding, fragrant and yellow, usually with maroon or purple spots, and flushed with purplish brown outside at the base. The thick segments vary in the degree to which they are recurved. There are a few stem roots. The stem reaches 50–180 cm (1 ft 8 in–6 ft) in height, with scattered, narrow to oval leaves. Germination – delayed hypogeal. Flowering time – early summer.

This lily, with its long-lasting flowers, looks lovely in a herbaceous border. It is lime-tolerant and can grow in a relatively heavy soil. It comes from north-east Turkey and the Caucasus, and prefers to be grown in a position that is shaded for at least part of the day.

L. nanum (*Nomocharis nana*) The solitary bell-shaped flowers are nodding and scented, pale purple to pink, and often dotted with brown or purple. It is not stem-rooting; the stem is 6–45 cm ($2\frac{1}{3}$– 18 in) tall, with very narrow, scattered leaves. Germination – immediate epigeal. Flowering time – early summer.

This lovely species from the Himalaya and western China (including Tibet) is suitable for the rock garden. It grows best in an acid soil and in light shade. Seed is freely produced and germinates well, but the seedlings usually grow slowly, and plants may take four or five years to flower.

Var. **flavidum** has pale yellow flowers.

L. nepalense This species has one to four more or less drooping, funnel-shaped flowers, sometimes with an unpleasant smell that is stronger at night. The segments are greeny white to pale greenish yellow, reddish outside and recurved at the tips. The bulb is stoloniferous. It is stem-rooting, the stem 70–100 cm (2 ft 4 in–3 ft) in height, with narrow, scattered leaves. Germination – immediate epigeal.

Lilium maculatum (see page 84)

Lilium nanum var. *flavidum* growing in the wild in Sikkim (see page 85)

or more, with leaves in whorls, and with some scattered ones towards the top of the stem. Germination – delayed hypogeal. Flowering time – mid summer.

This species does best in an acid soil with a lot of humus, and is questionably hardy. It is not easy to obtain and has been regarded as a lily for the specialist, though some gardeners maintain that it is not in fact a difficult species to grow.

L. oxypetalum (*Nomocharis oxypetala*) The flowers are usually solitary, broadly bell-shaped and outward-facing, yellow, often spotted with purple in the throat. Stem roots are absent; the stem reaches 20–30 cm (9–12 in), with narrow leaves that are scattered except for a whorl below the flower. Germination – immediate epigeal. Flowering time – early summer.

This species is more easily grown in northerly areas than southern ones; in the south it must be given more shade. A lovely species for the rock garden or raised bed. It is native to the north-west Himalaya.

Var. **insigne** has purple flowers.

L. papilliferum A rather unusual lily with one to three fragrant turk's-cap flowers. The segments are deep crimson-maroon,

Flowering time – late spring to mid summer.

This is an unusual and beautiful lily that should be tried more often; it is an interesting choice for a tub. The bulbs should be deeply planted in sharply drained acid soil with plenty of humus; in winter they should be covered with bracken or leafmould to protect them from frost. *L. nepalense* is native to Nepal, Bhutan and north India.

L. occidentale A lily that is rare both in the wild and in gardens. It comes from the west coast of the USA (Oregon and California). The nodding turk's-cap flowers usually number one to five, but there may be as many as 20. The segments vary in colour from crimson to orange-red with a green, yellow or orange base and purple-brown spots. The stems are 60–200 cm (2–6 ft) tall

paler at the base with pale warts, and tinged with green on the back. The bulb is stoloniform. It is stem-rooting, with the stem up to 90 cm (3 ft) tall and with narrow, scattered leaves. Germination – immediate epigeal. Flowering time – early to late summer. A rare species from south-west China that has never been common in gardens, it will grow in any well-drained soil and likes a position in dappled shade. It has some of the darkest flowers of any lily.

L. pardalinum (leopard lily, panther lily) An imposing species from the western USA (Oregon and California) that soon forms large clumps because of the branching habit of the bulb. There are up to ten nodding, turk's-cap flowers, which are often fragrant. Each segment is dark red in the upper part and orange to orange-red in the lower part, with maroon spots (some of which are encircled with yellow). The bulb is rhizomatous and branching. Stem roots are absent and the stem is 1.5–2.5 m (5–8 ft) tall, with the narrow leaves mostly in whorls. Germination – delayed hypogeal. Flowering time – mid summer.

This lily likes a soil with plenty of humus and sufficient moisture in the growing season. It is lime-tolerant. A place in sun or

light shade will suit it. Such a tall lily needs protection if the stems are not to be blown over or snapped by wind – planting it near shrubs will help, or it can be grown towards the back of a herbaceous border. It is good as a cut flower.

Var. **giganteum** is very vigorous, with stems up to 3 m (10 ft) bearing up to 50 crimson and yellow flowers that are densely spotted.

L. parryi A beautiful tall lily from the south-west USA (California and Arizona), which produces about 12, occasionally up to 50, scented, narrowly trumpet-shaped flowers. They are yellow, sometimes with dots of dark red or brown in the throat, and are outward-facing or drooping; each segment is recurved at the tip. The bulb is rhizomatous. The stem is 50–200 cm ($1\frac{1}{2}$–6 ft) tall, with narrow leaves that are mostly scattered. The stamens have orange-brown anthers. Germination – immediate hypogeal. Flowering time – mid summer.

In the wild, this lily is found with its bulbs in wet, sandy soil but its head in relatively dry air, and in gardens fungal

Lilium philadelphicum growing wild in New Hampshire, USA (see page 88)

Lilium nepalense (see page 85)

attack can be a nuisance. It is important, therefore, to plant it in a situation where there is moving air (though not high wind); stagnant air will encourage fungal disease. It grows best in dappled shade in a light, well-drained soil with plenty of humus. It is not one of the easiest lilies to grow, but can be very rewarding.

L. parvum A lily with up to 30 outward-facing, funnel-shaped flowers, which are red or crimson. Each segment usually has purple or deep red spots and is recurved at the tip. The bulb is rhizomatous; stem roots are lacking, the stem reaching as much as 2 m (6 ft) in height, bearing narrow leaves in whorls, or sometimes scattered. Germination – delayed hypogeal. Flowering time – mid summer.

This lily will grow in any soil, though it does like plenty of humus and sufficient water in the growing season. A semi-shady position suits it best. It comes from the western USA (Oregon and California) and is considered to be very closely related to L. maritimum.

L. philadelphicum (wood lily, flame lily, red lily) A species from eastern North America. The one or two, sometimes more, cup-shaped flowers face upwards and are deep yellow to orange-crimson, spotted with purple or maroon. Each segment is yellow towards the clawed base. The bulb is stoloniferous, but with very short stolons. Stem roots are present, the stem up to 1.25 m (4 ft) tall, with narrow leaves mostly in whorls. Germination – immediate or delayed epigeal, depending on the time of sowing. Flowering time – mid summer.

A pretty lily whose bulbs need protection from frost in winter, it grows best in an acid, light soil in sun or semi-shade, and needs moisture in the growing season.

L. philippinense As its name implies, this lily comes from the Philippines. The trumpet-shaped flowers are fragrant, outward-facing, usually one or two but occasionally up to six, white slightly flushed with green and sometimes purplish at the base outside; each segment is spreading at the tip. The bulb is stoloniferous. It is stem-rooting, with the stem 30–45 cm (1–1½ ft) tall, sometimes to 1 m (3 ft). The leaves are scattered and very narrow. Germination – immediate epigeal. Flowering time – mid summer.

This species is not hardy, and the bulbs should be planted at least 15 cm (6 in) deep in well-drained acid soil containing a lot of humus. It is lime-tolerant and grows best in light shade. Among lilies, L. philippinense has some of the longest flowers: they can be up to 25 cm (8 in) long.

L. pitkinense This species bears one to eight nodding, turk's-cap flowers, which are orange-red, yellow towards the centre and dotted with maroon. The bulb is rhizomatous. It is not stem-rooting; the stem is 1–2 m (3–6 ft) in height, with very narrow leaves that are scattered, but sometimes in whorls at the middle of the stem. Germination – delayed hypogeal. Flowering time – mid summer.

An extremely rare species in its native California, only found in a marshy area north of San Francisco, where it is now on the edge of extinction. It needs an acid soil with moisture (but not waterlogging) up to flowering time, and light shade.

L. polyphyllum This species has one to six, sometimes up to 30, very fragrant, pendent turk's-cap flowers, greenish white outside and creamy white inside streaked with green or purple. It is stem-rooting, with the stem 1–1.3 m (3–4 ft) tall. The leaves are narrow, usually scattered or with the lower ones in whorls. Germination – delayed hypogeal. Flowering time – early to mid summer.

This lily is from Afghanistan and the western Himalaya and is not common in gardens. Any soil will suit it provided that there is a lot of humus. It dislikes summer heat, so should be given a shady, north-facing position.

L. pomponium A lily from the Alpes Maritimes of France and Italy, where it grows on limestone. There are one to six, sometimes up to ten, nodding, unpleasantly smelling turk's-cap flowers that are bright red, marked with purplish or black lines and spots and with purplish warts. It is stem-rooting, the stem 20–100 cm (8–40 in) tall and bearing very narrow leaves. Germination – delayed epigeal. Flowering time – early summer. In gardens it will grow in acid soil as well as limy; it needs a sunny position.

L. pumilum (L. *tenuifolium*) This lily has nodding, slightly fragrant, turk's-cap flowers, usually two to seven, but occasionally up to 30. They are scarlet, often with a few black dots in the throat. It is stem-rooting, the stem 15–45 cm (6–18 in) tall, sometimes to 90 cm (3 ft), with very narrow, scattered leaves. Germination – immediate epigeal. Flowering time – early to mid summer.

A lovely species from eastern Asia, this lily has relatively small flowers. It produces a lot of seed and new plants are easily raised, generally flowering in three years. It grows best in full sun, in a non-limy, open and well-drained soil, with moisture in the growing season. It will make a bright patch in the rock garden or in the front of a herbaceous border, and is a useful species for pots or tubs.

Cultivars
'Golden Gleam' has flowers of apricot yellow and grows taller. 'Red Star' is now thought to be the result of a cross with L. *concolor*; it has outward-facing scarlet flowers with rather irregular, less reflexed segments.

L. pyrenaicum There are up to 12 pendent turk's-cap flowers, which smell rather nasty. They are yellow or greenish yellow, with purplish warts and deep purple lines and spots. It does not have stem roots. The stem, 30–135 cm (1–4½ ft) tall, bears narrow, scattered leaves that are hairless beneath. Germination – delayed epigeal. Flowering time – late spring to early summer.

A very hardy lily, easy to grow in any soil, in sun or dappled shade; it is naturalized in parts of Britain. It is useful because it

is one of the earliest lilies to flower. *L. pyrenaicum* itself comes from northern Spain and south-western France (including the Pyrenees).

There are several forms and varieties, some of which are in cultivation.
Forma **rubrum** ('Rubrum'), which is also found in the Pyrenees, has orange-red flowers, and 'Aureum' is a selected cultivar with deep yellow flowers.
Var. **albanicum** (L. *albanicum*, L. *carniolicum* subsp. *albanicum*) has yellow, unspotted flowers with warts, and leaf veins that are hairless beneath. It is native to southern Yugoslavia, Albania and northern Greece.
Var. **carniolicum** has red or orange spotted flowers with warts, and leaf veins that are densely downy beneath; it is native to the Alps and Yugoslavia.
Var. **jankae** (L. *jankae*, L. *carniolicum* subsp. *jankae*) has yellow flowers, with or without spots, but with warts, and leaf veins that are hairy beneath; it is found in north-west Italy and the northern Balkans.
Var. **ponticum** (L. *ponticum*, L. *carniolicum* subsp. *ponticum*, L. *georgicum*) has deep yellow flowers, striped and spotted with red-brown or purplish inside but lacking warts, and leaf veins that are downy beneath; it is a native of north-east Turkey.

L. regale A very beautiful lily from south-west China, with up to 25 or more powerfully fragrant, outward-facing, funnel-shaped flowers with a yellow throat; each segment is white, flushed with pinkish purple on the back and recurved at the tip. It is stem-rooting. The stem is 45–200 cm (1½–6 ft) tall, with very narrow, scattered leaves. Germination – immediate epigeal. Flowering time – early to mid summer.

It will grow in any good soil in sun or semi-shade. The young shoots may need protection from late frosts, but otherwise it is a strong, easy lily that should be tried in every garden.

Cultivars
'Album' has flowers that are almost white on the outside. 'Royal Gold' is a beautiful cultivar with yellow flowers, pinkish purple outside.

Lilium rubellum

L. rhodopaeum A native of Greece and Bulgaria that was discovered only some 35 years ago and is still fairly rare in gardens. There are one or two, sometimes up to five, nodding, funnel-shaped yellow flowers that are rather unpleasantly scented. The stamens have scarlet anthers which contrast attractively with the yellow segments. The stem is 80–100 cm (2½–3 ft) in height. The leaves are narrow, scattered, with a silvery, ciliate margin. Germination – unknown. Flowering time – early summer.

At the time of writing this species has not been raised from seed in cultivation, so no one knows how it germinates. However, seed has recently been offered through a specialist society, so this knowledge should soon become available. *L. rhodopaeum* should be grown in a sunny position.

L. rubellum A very pretty lily from Japan, which has up to nine broadly funnel-shaped, fragrant, outward-facing flowers; each segment is pink, often sprinkled with maroon dots at the base, the tip slightly recurved. It is stem-rooting, the stem 30–80 cm (1 ft–2 ft 8 in) in height, with scattered leaves that are narrowly oval with short stalks. Germination – delayed hypogeal. Flowering time – early summer.

L. rubellum grows best in a moist, acid soil in semi-shade, and looks lovely in a woodland garden; it is small enough to be grown in a rock garden or raised bed.

L. rubescens (redwood lily, chapparral lily) The trumpet-shaped flowers of this species are very fragrant, more or less erect and usually about 30 to a stem, although occasional plants have been known to produce 100! The segments are whitish at first but age to pinkish purple or purple, and sometimes have dark purple spots towards the base, recurved at the tips. The bulb is rhizomatous; there are no stem roots. The stem is usually up to 1.8 m (6 ft) tall, occasionally more, with narrow leaves usually in whorls. Germination – delayed hypogeal. Flowering time – mid summer.

This is a beautiful lily that is native to the western USA (California and Oregon) and not grown often enough, probably because it is not very easy. It needs a dry spell after flowering until the autumn, a need that can be difficult to satisfy. It does not have any fads regarding soil acidity, and should be tried in a sunny place. It is very similar to *L. washingtonianum*, and further study may show that these two species are one and the same.

L. sargentiae The fragrant, funnel-shaped flowers face outwards or droop slightly; usually there are two to five. The segments are white, pinkish, brown-purple or greenish on the back, and recurved at the tip. It is stem-rooting. The stem is 1–2 m (3–6 ft) tall, leafless at the base. The leaves are narrow and scattered, with bulbils in the axils. Germination – immediate epigeal. Flowering time – early to mid summer.

Not often seen in gardens, *L. sargentiae* does not like limy soils. It does best with its roots in the shade but its head in the sun. Some botanists have reported that the germination is delayed epigeal. It comes from western China.

L. sherriffiae A rare lily from Bhutan and Nepal that is not often grown. The narrowly bell-shaped flowers are usually solitary, deep brownish purple outside and chequered with dark yellow and green inside. It is stem-rooting, the stem 30–100 cm (1–3 ft) tall, bearing very narrow, scattered leaves. Germination – immediate

epigeal. Flowering time – late spring to early summer. It grows best in a peaty soil in northern areas, but nowhere is it long-lived, so seed should be saved. It is interesting in being the only lily with chequered flowers – a feature found in some fritillaries.

L. speciosum A species from Japan, China and Taiwan with very fragrant, pendent

Lilium sargentiae photographed growing in the wild in China

Lilium speciosum

turk's-cap flowers, usually up to 12 though as many as 40 can occur. Each segment is white or pale pink, flushed with deeper pink towards the base and with pink or crimson spots, and warty. Stem-rooting and the stem is 90–175 cm (3–5½ ft) in height, the leaves are scattered, narrowly oval with short stalks. Germination – delayed hypogeal. Flowering time – late summer to early autumn.

This lily needs good drainage and enough water in the growing season. It likes a shady place in a light soil with a lot of leafmould; it hates limy conditions. It is susceptible to virus diseases, and virus-free bulbs should be sought from specialist nurseries. It is a particularly good lily for growing in tubs or other containers, and for cutting; it also looks lovely in the herbaceous border.

Several varieties and cultivars are offered by nurserymen.

Var. *album* has white flowers, carried on a purplish stem.

Var. *gloriosoides* has segments that are white at the tip and base, crimson in the middle, and bear scarlet spots and warts.

Var. *magnificum* has rose-pink flowers spotted with crimson and borne on a purplish stem.

Var. *roseum* has rose-pink flowers and a green stem.

Var. *rubrum* has carmine-pink flowers and a purple-brown stem.

Cultivars

'Ellabee' has white segments with a central green vein, and brown anthers. 'Grand Commander' has flowers of lilac-purple, spotted with red, each segment margined with white. 'Lucie Wilson' has rose-pink flowers with red spots, and white edges to the segments. 'Melpomene' has dark red segments with white margins and very dark red warts. 'Uchida' is deep crimson-red, with tiny red dots.

L. sulphureum (L. *myriophyllum*) The flowers are fragrant, outward-facing or drooping. There are up to 15, and they are trumpet-shaped, cream to greenish white with a yellow throat, flushed pink outside, the segments recurved at the tips. It is stem-rooting. The stem is 1.5–2 m (4½–6 ft) tall, and the leaves are very narrow, scattered, with bulbils in the axils. Germination – immediate epigeal. Flowering time – late summer to early autumn. Not reliably hardy, this species is in most places best grown under glass. If grown outdoors, any well-drained soil will suit it, and it prefers light shade. It comes from south-west China and north Burma.

L. superbum This lily has up to 40 nodding, scented, turk's-cap flowers; each segment is orange, flushed with crimson especially at the tips, green at the base and with maroon spots. The bulb is stoloniferous. Stem-rooting, the stem is 1.5–3 m (5–10 ft) tall and bears narrowly oval leaves arranged mostly in whorls. Germination – delayed hypogeal. Flowering time – late summer to early autumn.

In its native eastern USA it generally grows in swampy places, but it does not want a swamp in gardens. It does best in an acid soil containing plenty of humus, and in a position in sun or partial shade. It can look beautiful in a woodland garden, and is useful for planting among shrubs such as rhododendrons, whose foliage can be dull once the flowers are over.

L. taliense A lily from south-west China that has up to 12 fragrant, pendent, turk's-cap flowers. The white segments have purple spots except at the tips, and the pollen is yellow. The bulb is stoloniferous. It is stem-rooting, the stem up to 1.2 m (4 ft) tall, with very narrow, scattered leaves. Germination – immediate epigeal. Flowering time – mid summer. It does best in an acid soil in semi-shade, but it is not long-lived in gardens. It was first introduced into cultivation in the 1930s by George Forrest.

L. tsingtauense Flowers one to six, sometimes more, cup-shaped, upward-facing, orange to orange-red, the segments rather thick, spotted with maroon and slightly warty. Stem-roots absent, the stem up to 1 m (3 ft) tall but usually less. The leaves are narrowly oval, mainly in whorls. Germination – delayed hypogeal. Flowering time – mid summer.

This species prefers an acid soil although it will grow in an alkaline one. It must have good drainage, and a lot of humus is beneficial. Full sun or semi-shade will suit it. It comes from Korea and eastern China.

L. vollmeri Nodding, turk's-cap flowers, usually one or two but sometimes more, deep orange with dark maroon spots. The bulb is rhizomatous. The stem is about 1 m (3 ft) tall with very narrow scattered leaves or some leaves in whorls. Germination – delayed hypogeal. Flowering time – mid summer. It is native to the western USA (Oregon and California) where it grows in what is probably the wettest habitat of any lily, inhabiting bogs and often in running water. However, in gardens it does not require such conditions but should be grown in a well-drained, humus-rich soil in a place that is shaded for part of the day.

L. wallichianum The one to four outward-facing, funnel-shaped flowers are fragrant; each segment is white or cream, tinged with yellow or greenish outside, and recurved at the tip. The bulb is stoloniferous. It is stem-rooting, with the stem up to 2 m (6 ft) in height and bearing very narrow, scattered leaves. Germination – immediate epigeal. Flowering time – early autumn.

This is a rare plant and a tender one, which needs a mild climate or can be grown under glass. Out of doors it must have a soil with plenty of grit, and seems to prefer a poor soil to a fertile one. It comes from the Himalaya.

L. wardii This lily can have up to 15 (sometimes up to 35) nodding, fragrant turk's-cap flowers. The segments are pink or purplish pink with purple or deep pink spots, and the pollen is orange. The bulb is stoloniform. It is stem-rooting, the stem up to 1.5 m (5 ft) tall, with narrow, scattered leaves. Germination – immediate epigeal. Flowering time – mid to late summer.

A beautiful lily that was introduced from Tibet by Frank Kingdon Ward and named after him. It is unfortunately susceptible to virus disease and so must constantly be raised from seed. It is not often seen, which is a pity. It likes a humus-rich soil and is not fussy about whether it is acid or alkaline, and it prefers a position in partial shade.

L. washingtonianum A lily from the western USA (Oregon and California) with scented flowers ranging from a few to 20 or more, facing outwards and funnel-shaped; each segment is white, turning lilac with age, dotted with purple towards the base and usually slightly recurved towards the tip. The bulb is stoloniferous. There are no stem roots; the stem is 1.2–2.5 m (4–8 ft) tall. The narrow, whorled leaves have wavy margins. Germination – delayed hypogeal. Flowering time – mid summer.

Not an easy lily in gardens – it seems to need a dry period in late summer and autumn, which is not natural in most areas – this lily likes an acid, peaty soil, and light shade suits it best.
Var. **minor** is not as tall and has white flowers, spotted with purple and not turning lilac as they age; the segments are narrower.
Var. **purpurascens** has flowers that are more cup-shaped, eventually ageing to wine-purple – it is a little more commonly seen in gardens than L. washingtonianum itself.

L. wigginsii The turk's-cap flowers are pendent, deep yellow with purple spots. It has a rhizomatous bulb. Stem roots are sometimes present, the stem is 90–120 cm (3–4 ft) tall. The leaves are very narrow, scattered or in whorls half way up the stem. Germination – delayed hypogeal. Flowering time – mid summer.

A western USA species from California and Oregon, where it grows in wettish places, it should be grown in an acid soil with a lot of humus, and sufficient moisture up to the time of flowering. It is not often seen in gardens, but seed or young bulbs are sometimes offered by the specialist societies.

*Cardiocrinum
giganteum*

CARDIOCRINUM

C. giganteum (*Lilium giganteum*) This is
the most commonly grown species, and
the tallest. The stem reaches 1.5–3.5 m (5–
11 ft) in height and bears leaves for the
whole length, from the basal rosette of
leaves to just below the flowers. Each stem
can carry up to 25 flowers, though there are
usually less than this. The flowers are
trumpet-shaped and droop slightly; they
are 15–20 cm (6–8 in) long, fragrant, pure
white outside and striped with reddish
purple inside. The lowest flowers usually
open first. Germination – epigeal, usually
delayed. Flowering time – early to mid
summer.

This spectacular plant comes from the
Himalaya, ranging from Kashmir to Tibet,
and north-west Burma. It was first discovered in the wild in 1821 and introduced
into cultivation in 1847, flowering five
years later.

Var. ***yunnanense*** is shorter, with a purple
stem that grows 1.5–2 m (5–6 ft) tall. The
flowers are often tinged with green, and

'Achilles'

those at the top of the stem open before the
lower ones. It comes from west and central
China. Recent research by Chinese botanists suggests that the features separating
var. *yunnanense* are not reliable and thus it is
not a 'good' distinct variety, but should be
included within *C. giganteum* itself.

C. cordatum (*Lilium cordatum, L.
cordifolium, Cardiocrinum glehnii*) Not
quite such a magnificent plant as *C.
giganteum* but still well worth having,
especially in a smaller garden. It is not, at
the moment, available commercially, and
so will have to be sought in the seed lists of
specialist societies. The stem grows 1.2–
2 m (4–6 ft) tall and does not have leaves in
the lower part. The basal leaves are in a
rosette, like those of *C. giganteum*. There
are usually four to ten flowers, sometimes
more, which are broadly trumpet-shaped,
fragrant and creamy white. The lower
segments have a yellow blotch and are
marked and spotted with reddish purple.

C. cordatum comes from Japan and the
Sakhalin Islands of the USSR. The young
leaves are an attractive brownish crimson
and emerge in early spring, so frost damage
may occur if they are not protected.

African Queen

Lily Cultivars

The number following the name of the grex or clone refers to the division into which it has been classified. See pages 72–4 and the classification chart on page 73 for further information.

'Achievement' II
Flowers turk's-cap, pale yellow, the segments thick and waxy, and with orange pollen. Height 1–1.2 m (3–4 ft). Early summer. A hybrid between *L. martagon* and *L. hansonii* that increases quickly.

'Achilles' I(a)
Flowers cup-shaped, upward-facing, yellow with dark spots. Height about 1 m (3 ft). Late summer.

'Admiral' I(a)
Flowers cup-shaped, upward-facing, tangerine-orange with chocolate-brown spots towards the centre. Height about 1 m (3 ft). Early summer.

African Queen IV(a)
The flowers are scented, trumpet-shaped, yellow to orange inside and brownish outside. Height about 1.5–2 m (5–6 ft). Mid to late summer. A beautiful selection from the Aurelian Hybrids, with pyramids of drooping flowers. It can be grown in semi-shade.

'Afterglow' IV
The rich crimson flowers are heavily spotted with maroon and contrast well with the yellow throat. Height 1.5–2 m (5–6 ft). Early to mid summer. A rapidly increasing lily selected from the Bellingham Hybrids (see page 96). It is especially good as a cut flower.

Albino Hybrids V
Flowers funnel-shaped, white with a greenish centre. Pollen deep yellow or orange. Height up to 1.5 m (5 ft). The plants will flower six months after the seeds are sown.

'Allegra' VII(d)
Flowers fragrant, about 20 cm (8 in) across, white with sparse pink or white warts on at least some of the recurved, ruffled segments. The pollen is brown. Height 1.5–2 m (5–6 ft). Late summer. An impressive cultivar involving *L. auratum* and varieties of *L. speciosum* in its parentage, and bearing up to 25 flowers.

'Alpenglow' I(a)
Flowers cup-shaped, upward-facing, rose-pink fading to purplish pink, yellow in the throat and spotted with magenta. Height about 1 m (3 ft). Early summer. Sometimes listed in catalogues as 'Alpine Glow'.

'Amber Gold' I(c)
Turk's-cap flowers that are pendent, orange-yellow, spotted with maroon in the centre and with red-brown anthers. Height 1.2–1.5 m (4–5 ft). Early to mid summer. A beautiful, unusually tall selection from the Fiesta Hybrids.

'Angela North' I(c)
Drooping flowers, slightly scented, five to seven per stem, dark pinkish red with some darker spots, segments recurved. Height 50–120 cm (1½–4 ft). Mid summer.

'Apricot Beauty' I(b)
Flowers outward-facing, orange becoming orange-red in the centre and with many dark spots. Height about 1 m (3 ft). Mid to late summer.

'Ariadne' I(c)
A hybrid involving *L. lankongense*. Flowers pendent, scented, pale orange, each segment flushed with purple at the tip. Mid summer. Each stem carries 20 to 30 small flowers.

'Aristo' see **'Orange Aristo'**

'Attila' I(b)
Flowers outward-facing, orange-yellow, with brownish purple spots. Height 60–100 cm (2–3 ft). Mid summer.

Aurelian Hybrids VI(a)
A grex derived from *L. sargentiae*, *L. henryi* and *L. leucanthum*, from which many clones have been selected and named. Flowers trumpet-shaped, white, pink, yellow or apricot, outward-facing or drooping. Height 1.2–1.5 m (4–5 ft). Mid summer. Superb lilies for mass planting, or for growing in groups in the herbaceous border.

'Avignon' I(a)
Flowers upward-facing, about eight per stem, orange-red, the segments with the tips slightly recurved. Height about 1 m (3 ft). Mid summer.

'Barbara North' I(c)
Flowers slightly scented, mid pink with a paler pink throat. Each recurved segment has some small, dark red spots. Height 70–120 cm (2 ft 4 in–4 ft). Mid summer. Each stem carries about 10 flowers.

'Beckwith Tiger' I(c)
Flowers yellow spotted with purple, the tips of the segments strongly recurved. Height 1.4–1.5 m (4½–5 ft). Mid summer. A hybrid of *L. leichtlinii*.

Bellingham Hybrids IV
A grex produced from hybridization between *L. humboldtii*, *L. pardalinum* and *L. parryi*. The flowers, often up to 20 per stem. They range from yellow to orange-red, and many have brown or red spots. Height 2–2.2 m (6–7 ft). Early to mid summer. These easily grown lilies are good for cutting and prefer a position in semi-shade on an acid soil. The bulbs increase rapidly.

Bellmaid Hybrids IV
Flowers golden yellow flushed with orange, usually turning red with age. These hybrids are derived from the Bellingham Hybrids.

'Bingo' I(b)
Flowers outward-facing, orange-red, the segments slightly recurved. Stems 40–50 cm (about 1½ ft) tall. Early to mid summer. A short lily for the front of a border or a tub.

'Black Beauty' VII(d)
Flowers very dark red with a green centre; each recurved segment is margined with white. Height 1.2–2 m (4–6 ft) Mid summer. An easy-to-grow clone, which has *L. speciosum* and *L. henryi* as its parents.

'Black Dragon' VI(a)
Flowers trumpet-shaped, scented, white inside, the outside dark red; 12 or more flowers are carried on a stem. Height 1.5–2 m (5–6 ft). Mid summer. A magnificent lily for beginners, it has *L. leucanthum* in its parentage and always attracts attention. It looks very fine grown in a tub.

'Black Magic' VI(a)
Flowers fragrant, trumpet-shaped, white inside and purple-brown outside, opening from maroon buds. Height 1.2–2 m (4–6 ft) or more. Mid to late summer.

'Bonfire' VII(b)
Flowers bowl-shaped, with crimson spots, deep crimson inside, silvery white outside, flushed with shell pink; each segment has a silver edge. Height 1.2–1.5 m (4–5 ft). Late summer.

'Bora' I(a)
Flowers upward-facing, deep pink, the throat pale yellow with a few maroon dots. Height about 1 m (3 ft). Early summer.

'Brandywine' I(b)
Flowers outward-facing, orange with orange-red spots, the segments slightly recurved. Height 1–1.2 m (3–4 ft). Early to mid summer. A free-flowering lily selected from the Mid-Century Hybrids.

'Bright Beauty' I(a)
Upward-facing, deep yellow flowers with orange-brown spots and blotches in the throat and greenish yellow nectary fur-rows. The pollen is orange-brown. Height about 1.2 m (4 ft). Mid summer. The stems carry about 30 flowers and are tinged with red.

'Bright Star' VI(d)
Scented, outward-facing, flattish, white flowers, each segment recurved at the tip with a central orange stripe giving the effect of an orange star. Height 1–1.5 m (3–5 ft). Mid summer. A selection from the Aurelian Hybrids that is easy to grow. It will grow on limy soils.

Bronzino Strain I(c)
Nodding flowers with reflexed segments, ranging from orange-yellow to chocolate-brown. Some plants have flowers of two colours. Stem 1.2–1.5 m (4–5 ft), carrying up to 40 flowers. Early to mid summer. This grex was selected from the Fiesta Hybrids.

Bullwood Hybrids IV
Variously spotted flowers, and ranging from peach and orange to deep red. Height to 3 m (10 ft). *L. pardalinum* is one of the parents.

Burgundy Strain I(c)
Nodding turk's-cap flowers, cherry-red, claret or burgundy. Height 1–1.2 m (3–4 ft). Mid summer. The flowers are long-lasting and stand up well to hot sun. This grex was derived from the Fiesta Hybrids (see page 101).

'Camborne' I(b)
Flowers bright orange-red and outward-facing. Stems about 1 m (3 ft) tall. Early summer. A cross between *L. lancifolium* and 'Enchantment'.

'Cambridge' I(c)
Flowers upward-facing, deep red, each segment yellowish pink at the tip and base and with black spots. Height 30–35 cm (12–14 in). Mid summer. A short lily useful for pots or the front of a border.

'Capri' I(a)
Upward-facing flowers, ivory white in-

'Bright Star' (see page 97)

Throat orange with deep magenta-brown spots. Height 2 m (6 ft). Mid summer.

'Chinook' I(a)
Upward-facing flowers, pale apricot-buff. Height about 1.2 m (4 ft). Early to mid summer.

'Cinnabar' I(a)
Flowers cup-shaped, upward-facing, maroon, speckled in the centre. Height 1–1.2 m (3–4 ft). Early to mid summer. A good lily for forcing. Selected from the popular Mid-Century Hybrids.

Citronella Strain I(c)
Flowers pendent, turk's-cap, up to 30 per stem, lemon yellow to golden yellow, spotted with black or maroon. Height 1.2–1.5 m (4–5 ft). Mid summer. Lilies of this grex are vigorous and long-lasting; they are selections from the Fiesta Hybrids.

'Cocktail' I(a)
Flowers cup-shaped, upward-facing, rose-pink with orange-buff blotches in the throat and brown spots. Height about 1.2 m (4 ft). Early summer.

side, pale yellow outside, with a greenish centre and green tips to the segments. The nectary furrows are purple and the pollen is orange-brown. Height 1–1.2 m (3–4 ft). Mid summer.

Carnival Strain VI(c)
Flowers pendent, with reflexed segments, in white and shades of yellow and apricot. Mid summer. An attractive group of lilies selected from the Aurelian Hybrids.

'Casa Blanca' VII(b)
Flattish white flowers with warts in the throat. The segments are recurved at the tips and the orange-red pollen makes a most attractive contrast. Height about 1 m (3 ft). Mid summer to early autumn.

'Cherrywood' IV
Flowers strong red when grown in sun but reddish orange when grown in shade.

'Connecticut King'

'Casa Blanca'

'Colleen' I(a)
Cream flowers fading to white, and slightly tinged with green on the outside. Each segment is dotted with magenta-purple towards the base. The pollen is orange-brown. Height about 1 m (3 ft). Early to mid summer. The stems bear 8 to 20 upward-facing flowers. A hybrid between 'Sterling Star' and 'Connecticut King'.

'Concorde' I(a)
Flowers upward-facing, lemon yellow, somewhat greenish in the throat and speckled with small brown-red spots. The pollen is orange. Height 60–100 cm (2–3 ft). Early to mid summer.

'Connecticut Beauty' I(a)
Flowers cup-shaped, upward-facing, yellow shaded darker along the centre of each segment and spotted in the centre. Height 60–100 cm (2–3 ft). Early to mid summer. 'Medaillon' (often misspelt 'Medallion') is considered to be the same clone.

'Connecticut King' I(a)
Flowers upward-facing, deep yellow, slightly paler at the tips of the segments. Height 1 m (3 ft). Early to mid summer. A vigorous grower that is useful for pots or tubs and as a cut flower. One of its parents is *L. lancifolium* var. *flaviflorum*.

'Connecticut Lemonglow' I(b)
Flowers outward-facing, pure unspotted yellow. Height about 1.5 m (5 ft). Mid summer.

'Connecticut Yankee' I(c)
Nodding, orange-red flowers with a few dark spots, 8 to 20 per stem. Height 1.2–2 m (4–6 ft). Mid summer. Vigorous and dependable.

Copper King Strain VI(a)
Flowers fragrant, trumpet-shaped, golden yellow, tinted orange. Height 1.2–2 m (4–6 ft). Mid summer. A grex selected from the Golden Clarion Strain, which does well in semi-shade.

'Corina' I(a)
Flowers upward-facing, red with dark brown dots in the centre. Height 60–100 cm (2–3 ft). Early summer. One of the best modern reds. 'Cinnabar' is one of its parents.

'Corsage' I(b)
Flowers outward-facing, pale pink, dotted with maroon, the centre white, the outside rose-pink and cream. The recurved segments are rather thick. Stems about 1.2 m (4 ft) tall bearing 12 or more long-lasting flowers, ideal for cutting. Mid summer.

'Damson' VI(a)
Flowers trumpet-shaped, glistening plum-purple. Height 1.2–1.5 m (4–5 ft). Mid summer. To obtain this lily, Aurelian Hybrids were crossed with selections from *L. leucanthum*.

'Destiny' I(a)
Flowers upward-facing, yellow with brown spots, each segment reflexed at the tip. Height 1–1.2 m (3–4 ft). Early summer. A vigorous and free-flowering lily that is useful for growing in pots.

'Discovery' I(c)
Nodding, pinkish lilac, turk's-cap flowers, the centre paler and spotted with dark crimson, the outside pink with a silvery sheen. Brown anthers are borne on pink filaments. Height 60–100 cm (2–3 ft). Mid summer. Sixteen or more flowers are carried in a pyramidal flowerhead. One of the parents is *L. amabile* var. *luteum*.

'Dominique' VII(c)
Flowers red-purple, with spots in the throat and yellow-green nectary furrows. The segments have slightly ruffled margins. The pollen is a contrasting orange-red. Height about 40 cm (16 in). Mid summer. A short lily useful for containers or the front of a border.

'Duet' I(a)
Primrose yellow flowers, suffused and streaked with darker yellow. Each segment has a pale green midrib on the outside and an orange-brown nectary furrow. The pollen is orange. Height about 1 m (3 ft). Early summer. Each stem carries 11 or 12 cup-shaped, upward-facing flowers.

'Dukat' I(c)
Flowers outward-facing, orange-yellow, each segment darker at the tip and with deep crimson spots towards the base. Pollen brown. Height 30–60 cm (1–2 ft). Mid summer. A short-growing clone that can be planted at the front of a border.

'Edith' I(a)
Flowers upward-facing, about 15 cm (6 in) across, cream inside with some black spots at the centre, pale yellow outside. The nectary furrows are green and the pollen is brown. Stem about 1.2 m (4 ft) tall, carrying 8 to 25 flowers. Mid summer.

'Empress of India' VII(b)
Flowers bowl-shaped, deep rich red, the segments edged in white and with prominent warts towards the base. Eight to ten flowers, 25 cm (10 in) across, are borne on the stems, which attain 1.2–1.5 m (4–5 ft). Late summer.

'Enchantment' I(a)
A selection from the Mid-Century Hybrids. Flowers upward-facing, cup-shaped, orange-red with black spots. Height 60–100 cm (2–3 ft). Early summer. The stems can carry up to 16 flowers. A wonderful and reliable lily for growing in a tub or for creating a splash of colour in the herbaceous border. Good for beginners and for use as a cut flower.

'Eros' I(c)
Turk's-cap flowers, nodding, pink and scented. Height 1–1.2 m (3–4 ft). Mid summer. An easily grown lily.

'Eurovision' I(a)
Orange flowers, upward-facing, cup-shaped, the throat flushed red. The nectary furrows are violet-red. Height about 1.2 m (4 ft). Mid summer. The stems usually carry about nine flowers.

Everest Strain VII(d)
Fragrant flowers, white with green centres and spotted with maroon, each segment heavy-textured and crinkled. Stems 1.5–2 m (5–6 ft), carrying up to 14 flowers. Mid to late summer. *L. speciosum* and *L. auratum* are among the parents.

'Exception' I(b)
Flowers outward-facing, deep pink with maroon spots, fading to white towards the centre of each recurved segment. Some or all of the filaments are flattened and look like the segments, giving the flower a most unusual appearance. Height 1–1.2 m (3–4 ft). Mid summer. This lily does not produce any pollen. It is a hybrid between *L. cernuum* and *L. davidii*.

'Falmouth' I(c)
Flowers spotted, orange-red. Height about 80 cm (2½ ft). Early summer.

'Festival' I(a)
Flowers upward-facing, light orange with a central deep red star and brown spots, the segments with red edges and tips. The outside of the flower is red-brown to purple-red. The anthers are orange. Height 1 m (3 ft). Early to mid summer.

'Feuerzauber' I(a)
Flowers upward-facing, cup-shaped, orange-red, each segment recurved at the tip. Height 45–60 cm (1½–2 ft). Early to mid summer. A strong grower, good for forcing and for growing in pots or tubs. *L. lancifolium* is one of its parents.

Fiesta Hybrids I(c)
Nodding flowers ranging from pale yellow to bright red, spotted with maroon. Height about 1.2 m (4 ft). Early to mid summer. Derived from crosses between *L. amabile*, *L. dauricum* and *L. davidii*. The plants grow best in a sunny position and are suitable for growing in tubs and for cutting.

'Fire King' I(b)
Outward-facing, widely funnel-shaped flowers, reddish orange, spotted with brown-purple; each segment is reflexed at the tip. Height 1–1.2 m (3–4 ft). Mid summer. Looks good grown in pots or tubs. Vigorous with up to 20 flowers per stem.

'Firecracker' I(a)
Flowers upward-facing, deep cherry red. Height 1–1.2 m (3–4 ft). Early to mid summer. The flowers do not fade in full sun.

'First Love' VI(b)
Flowers bowl-shaped, outward-facing, slightly fragrant, the throat pale green, segments pink on the edges, golden yellow in the centre. Height 1.5–2 m (5–6 ft). Early to mid summer.

'Fuga' I(c)
Flowers nodding, turk's-cap, up to 18 per stem, bright orange, with dark raised spots. Height 1–2 m (3–6 ft). Early to mid summer. A hybrid between *L. cernuum* and *L. davidii*.

'Furore' VII(c)
Flowers flat, white with white warts on the inside, each segment with a pale yellow stripe outside. Pollen red-brown. Height about 1.2 m (4 ft). Late summer.

'Gold Medal' I(a)
Upward-facing, cup-shaped flowers, yellow, flushed with deeper yellow in the centre. Height 80–100 cm (2½–3 ft). Early to mid summer.

Golden Chalice Hybrids I(a)
Flowers cup-shaped, upward-facing, with broad segments in various shades of yellow. Some have spotted flowers. Height 1–2 m (3–6 ft). Late spring to early summer. An early flowering grex, useful for starting the lily season.

Golden Clarion Strain VI(a)
Trumpet-shaped flowers, yellow to golden brown, often with dark red shading, especially on the outside. Stems with up to 15 flowers, up to 2.1 m (7 ft). Mid summer. A vigorous and reliable grex, suitable for beginners, selected from the Aurelian Hybrids.

'Golden Melody' I(a)
Flowers cup-shaped, upward-facing, yellow-orange with a greenish throat and red-brown spots in the centre. Anthers deep red-brown. Height 1–1.2 m (3–4 ft). Mid summer.

'Green Dragon'

'Golden Souvenir' I(b)

Flowers are outward-facing, yellow with purple spots. Height about 1 m (3 ft). Mid to late summer. *L. lancifolium* and *L. × hollandicum* are involved in the parentage.

Golden Splendor Strain VI(a)

Flowers scented, trumpet-shaped, outward-facing, in various shades of yellow, each segment with a dark red stripe on the back. Height 1.2–2 m (4–6 ft). Mid summer. A vigorous grex selected from the Aurelian Hybrids, with strong, sturdy stems. These lilies look lovely in large pots or tubs.

Golden Sunburst Strain VI(a)

Flowers widely funnel-shaped, golden yellow, with warts in the centre. Height 1.2–2 m (4–6 ft). Mid to late summer. The stems bear 8 to 20 flowers, which are good for cutting.

'Green Dragon' VI(a)

Fragrant flowers, widely trumpet-shaped, white, stained chartreuse green outside, the anthers deep yellow. Height 1.5–2.2 m (5–7¼ ft). Mid summer. This lily can be planted in semi-shade and does well in

large pots. It was selected from the Olympic Hybrids.

Green Magic Strain VI(a)

Flowers 8 to 20 per stem, trumpet-shaped, white, and green in the centre. The pollen is brown-red. Height 1–2 m (3–6 ft). Mid summer.

Hallmark Strain I(c)

Flowers turk's-cap, nodding, white dotted with dark red, and with red anthers. Height 1–1.2 m (3–4 ft). Mid summer. The parents are *L. cernuum* and *L. lancifolium*. There are 15 to 20 flowers per stem, and they are long-lasting even in hot sun.

Harlequin Strain I(c)

Flowers pendent, turk's-cap, spotted, occurring in almost all the colours found in lilies. Height 1–1.5 m (3–5 ft). Mid summer. This grex, which was selected from the Mid-Century Hybrids, is vigorous, very hardy and reliable; the plants should be grown in a sunny place, and look lovely in a herbaceous border. They are also useful for cut flowers.

'Harmony' I(a)

Upward-facing flowers, orange with small maroon spots and broad segments with reflexed tips. Height 45–100 cm (1½–3 ft). Mid summer. A good lily for cutting, this is a clone selected from the Mid-Century Hybrids.

Opposite: 'Lady Bowes Lyon' (see page 105)

Right: 'Eros' (see page 100)

Heart's Desire Strain VI(b)
Between 15 and 20 flowers per stem, widely bowl-shaped, outward-facing to drooping, white, cream or yellow, often orange in the throat. Height 1.2–2 m (4–6 ft). Mid summer. A grex derived from the Aurelian Hybrids.

'Honeydew' VI(a)
Flowers narrowly trumpet-shaped, greenish yellow, each pointed segment with a green stripe on the back. Height 1–1.5 m (3–5 ft). Mid summer. There are up to 15 flowers on each sturdy stem. The orange anthers contrast beautifully with the greenish yellow segments.

'Hornback's Gold' I(c)
Flowers large, soft yellow with light spotting. Height about 1.2 m (4 ft). Mid summer.

Imperial Crimson VII(c)
Flowers flat, scented, deep crimson, each segment with a white margin. The pollen is red. Height about 1.5 m (5 ft). Late summer. A grex involving *L. auratum* and *L. speciosum*.

Imperial Gold VII(c)
Flowers flat, scented, white, each segment with a central yellow band and spotted with maroon, recurved at the tip. The pollen is red. Height about 2 m (6 ft). Late summer. A grex derived from *L. auratum* and *L. speciosum*.

Imperial Silver VII(c)
Flowers flat, scented, up to 25 cm (10 in) across, white, dotted with dark red, on stems 1.5–2 m (5–6 ft) tall. The pollen is orange-red. Late summer. A grex with *L. auratum* and *L. speciosum* in the parentage.

'Inferno' I(a)
Flowers cup-shaped, orange, with dark dots in the centre, 8 to 12 per stem. Height 60–80 cm (2–2½ ft). Early to mid summer.

'Iona' I(c)
Flowers orange, with strongly recurved segments that are paler at the tips and spotted with red in the lower two thirds of the bloom. Height about 1.5 m (5 ft). Mid summer.

'Ivory Queen' I(c)
Flowers ivory white with grey-brown spots in the throat and with orange pollen. Height 1.2–1.5 m (4–5 ft). Mid summer.

'Jacques S. Dijt' II
Turk's-cap flowers, up to 20 on a stem, creamy yellow with purple spots, and orange-red pollen. Height 1.2–2 m (4–6 ft). Early to mid summer. *L. martagon* var. *album* and *L. hansonii* were used to produce this clone.

Jamboree Strain VII(d)
Fragrant flowers, crimson with darker spots, the segments recurved, with narrow, often crinkled white margins. Stems 1–2 m (3–6 ft). Late summer. A vigorous grex derived from crosses between *L. auratum* and *L. speciosum*; mature plants carry 14 or more flowers on each stem. This lily looks lovely grown in tubs.

'Jetfire' I(a)
Flowers cup-shaped, upward-facing, orange-red with a yellow throat. The tips of the segments are slightly recurved. Height 90–120 cm (3–4 ft). Early to mid summer. The stems carry 6 to 12 flowers. The parents are *L.* × *hollandicum* and 'Connecticut King'.

'Joan Evans' I(a)
Flowers upward-facing, cup-shaped, orange to golden yellow with maroon spots in the centre. The broad segments curve backwards and the anthers are dark red. Height about 1 m (3 ft). Mid summer. A clone selected from the Mid-Century Hybrids.

'Joanna' I(a)
Flowers cup-shaped, bright yellow, spotted with brown in the centre, each segment flushed with deep gold in the middle. Pollen brown. Height about 1.4 m (4½ ft). Early to mid summer. A hybrid of 'Connecticut King'.

'Journey's End' VII(d)
Flowers deep pink, spotted with maroon, each segment slightly reflexed and white at the edges and tip. Height 1–2 m (3–6 ft). Late summer.

'Joy' VII(b)
Up to six flowers per stem, upward-facing, red-purple with maroon spots towards the centre, and red-brown pollen. Height about 70 cm (2 ft 4 in). Mid summer.

'Juliana' I(a)
Cup-shaped flowers, cream fading to white and slightly spotted. Height about 1 m (3 ft). Mid summer.

'Karen North' I(c)
Flowers orange-pink with a few dark pink spots; each segment has a dark central stripe on the outside. The pollen is dark brown. Height up to about 1.4 m (4½ ft). Mid summer. The dark red stems carry 16 to 20 flowers.

'King Pete' I(b)
Flowers outward-facing, very broadly cup-shaped, cream marked with orange on the central part of each segment, spotted. The pollen is dark orange. Height 60–100 cm (2–3 ft). Mid summer. A strong, long-lasting, attractive lily, produced by crossing 'Connecticut King' with the Panamint Strain. A good lily for cutting.

'Lady Ann' VI(b)–(c)
Flowers trumpet-shaped, creamy yellow flushed with orange in the throat. Pollen brownish maroon. Height 1.5 m (5 ft). Mid to late summer.

'Lady Bowes Lyon' I(c)
Nodding, turk's-cap flowers, red, spotted with black, the segments reflexed. Height 1–1.2 m (3–4 ft). Mid summer.

'Ladykiller' I(a)
Flowers upward-facing, cup-shaped, the recurved segments orange with dark red spots. Height about 1 m (3 ft). Early summer. Produced by crossing *L. lancifolium* with 'Harmony'.

'Lake Tahoe' IV
Red flowers spotted with pinkish red, the throat white with gold bands and green in the very centre, the segments reflexed. The pollen is dark brown. Height 2 m (6 ft) or more. Mid summer. *L. bolanderi* is one of the parents.

'Lake Tulare' IV
Flowers pink, white in the centre, spotted with dark red, the segments reflexed. The pollen is brown. Height 2 m (6 ft) or more. Mid summer. A graceful lily that looks good grown among protective shrubs. It is a cross between the Bullwood Hybrids and *L. bolanderi*.

'Langtry' I(c)
Flowers yellow, spotted with maroon, the segments strongly recurved. The pollen is dark brown. Height about 1 m (3 ft) Mid summer. The stems bear bulbils in the leaf axils. *L. leichtlinii* played a part in the parentage.

'Laura' VII(d)
Flowers various shades of pinkish purple with darker spots. Each recurved segment has a reddish stripe, a whitish tip, and a paler, lightly ruffled margin. The nectary furrows are lime green and the pollen is rust brown. Height 1–1.5 m (3–5 ft). Late summer.

'Limelight' VI(a)
Trumpet-shaped, slightly drooping flowers, fragrant, yellow with a hint of green. Height 1–2 m (3–6 ft). Mid summer. A lovely clone for the herbaceous border.

'Mabel Violet' VI(a)
Flowers up to 15 per stem, trumpet-shaped, dark pink inside with a greenish throat, maroon-pink outside. The pollen is maroon-brown. Height 1–1.2 m (3–4 ft). Mid summer. It arose from a cross between plants of the Pink Pearl Trumpets and the Pink Perfection Strain, made in 1970. It is a strong growing lily. The superb and unusual coloration is guaranteed to attract comment.

'Iona' (see page 104)

'Manuella' I(a)
Flowers cup-shaped, upward-facing, dusky reddish pink with brownish black spots. Height about 1 m (3 ft). Early summer. A cross between 'Ladykiller' and *L. cernuum*.

'Marhan' II
A hybrid between *L. martagon* var. *album* and *L. hansonii*. Flowers turk's-cap, nodding, the recurved orange segments with red-brown spots. Stem 1.5–2 m (5–6 ft). Early summer.

'Marie North' I(c)
Slightly scented flowers, whitish, suffused with pale mauvish pink, darker in the centre, opening from dark buds. The segments are strongly recurved and have dark red spots confined mainly to the central area. Height 70–120 cm (2 ft 4 in–4 ft). Mid summer. Bulbils are sometimes produced in the leaf axils.

'Marilyn Monroe' I(a)
Cup-shaped, upward-facing flowers,

butter yellow and unspotted. Anthers brown. Height about 60 cm (2 ft). Mid summer. A dwarf lily suitable for the front of a border.

'Matchless' I(a)
Flowers cup-shaped, upward-facing, orange-red, the segments slightly recurved. Stems 1–1.5 m (3–5 ft), dark purple-brown and bearing 5 to 15 flowers. Mid summer.

'Maxwill' I(c)
Nodding flowers, orange-red, spotted with black, anthers brick-red. Stems 1.5–2.2 m (5–7 ft) carrying 30 flowers or more. Mid summer. The name is derived from the two varieties that were used as parents – *L. leichtlinii* var. *maximowiczii* and *L. davidii* var. *willmottiae*.

'Medaillon' see **'Connecticut Beauty'**

Mid-Century Hybrids I(a)
Upward-facing flowers, in a range of

yellows, oranges and reds. Height 60–100 cm (2–3 ft). Early to mid summer. An easily grown, vigorous grex produced by crossing *L. lancifolium* with *L. × hollandicum*, and containing many fine lilies. They like to be planted in a sunny place, and are suitable for a herbaceous border. They also make fine cut flowers.

'Minos' I(c)
Nodding flowers with red, reflexed segments. Stem 1–1.2 m (3–4 ft) tall, bearing 12 to 20 flowers, and with bulbils in the leaf axils.

'Mont Blanc' I(a)
Upward-facing flowers, white with a few spots in the centre. Height about 60 cm (2 ft). Early to mid summer. A long-lasting lily that was produced in 1978.

'Montreux' I(a)
Cup-shaped flowers, pink with brown dots in the throat. Pollen buff-yellow. Height about 1 m (3 ft). Mid summer.

Moonlight Strain VI(a)
Trumpet-shaped flowers, greenish yellow. Height 1.2–2 m (4–6 ft). Mid summer. A robust and beautiful grex, suitable for growing in a herbaceous border.

'Moulin Rouge' I(b)
Flowers outward-facing, orange-red, veined and blotched with orange and speckled with dark brown. Height about 1 m (3 ft). Mid summer. Long-lasting and a good subject for forcing.

'Mrs R.O. Backhouse' II
Turk's-cap flowers, pale brownish yellow with reddish spots, the outside flushed with magenta; segments reflexed. Height 1.2–2 m (4–6 ft). Early summer. Up to 20 flowers per stem are borne in a pyramidal flowerhead. A vigorous lily produced by crossing *L. hansonii* and *L. martagon*.

'Nightingale' IV
Flowers nodding, fragrant, turk's-cap, clear lilac with a splash of orange in the centre of each segment, and spotted with dark red. Height 1.2–1.5 m (4–5 ft). Early to mid summer. A lily whose complex parentage includes *L. kelloggii* and *L. pardalinum*.

'Lake Tulare' (see page 105)

Pink Perfection Strain (see page 109)

'Odysseus' I(b)
Flowers outward-facing, orange. Height 1–1.2 m (3–4 ft). The stems carry about 10 flowers and produce bulbils in the leaf axils.

Olympic Hybrids VI(a)
Flowers trumpet-shaped, fragrant, varying from white and cream through yellow and greenish to pink, usually yellow in the throat; each segment pink or purplish on the back. Height 1.2–2 m (4–6 ft). Mid summer. A grex of vigorous lilies derived from crosses involving *L. sargentiae*, *L. leucanthum*, *L. brownii* and *L. sulphureum*.

'Omega' VII
Five or six flowers per stem, with rose-pink, slightly recurved segments edged with white. The throat is pale yellow and spotted with red. Pale green pollen. Height 60–75 cm (2–2½ ft). Late summer.

'Orange Aristo' I(a)
Cup-shaped flowers, light orange with red-brown spots. Anthers brown. Height about 60 cm (2 ft). Early to mid summer. Sometimes listed as 'Aristo' in catalogues.

'Orange Triumph' I(a)
Cup-shaped, upward-facing flowers, orange, spotted with dark purple. Height about 1.2 m (4 ft). Mid summer. There are about 12 flowers per stem.

'Orestes' I(b)
Flowers outward-facing, orange-red, segments reflexed. Stems bearing 12 to 18 flowers, and with bulbils in the leaf axils. Height 1–1.2 m (3–4 ft). Mid summer.

Oriental Hybrids VII(b)
Very fragrant, bowl-shaped flowers in scarlet and reds. Mid summer to early autumn. A grex derived mainly from *L. auratum* and *L. speciosum*. These lilies appreciate regular feeding.

Paisley Strain II
Turk's-cap flowers in shades of purple, orange-yellow or mahogany red, all dotted with maroon. Height 1–1.5 m (3–5 ft).

Early summer. Derived from a cross between *L. martagon* var. *album* and *L. hansonii*. Can stand a little lime in the soil, and will grow happily in semi-shade.

'Pan' I(c)
Scented, white, nodding flowers. Height 1–1.2 m (3–4 ft). Mid summer. A clone whose very complex parentage involves *L. lankongense* and *L. lancifolium*.

Panamint Strain I(c)
Large, nodding flowers of cream and ivory white with a green flush in the throat, the thick segments sprinkled with tiny red dots. Height 1.2–1.3 m (4–4½ ft). Mid summer. The flowers are long-lasting.

'Pandora' I(a)
Flowers upward-facing, cup-shaped, pale orange, 18 to 20 on a stem. Height about 60 cm (2 ft). Early summer.

'Papillon' I(a)
Flowers cup-shaped, upward-facing, red with an orange-yellow throat that has a few spots. The nectary furrows are greenish. Height about 90 cm (3 ft). Mid summer. The stems are tinged with red and carry about 22 flowers.

'Paprika' I(b)
Deep crimson-red, outward-facing flowers. Height 45–100 cm (1½–3 ft). Mid summer. A selection from the Mid-Century Hybrids – good for forcing.

'Peachwood' IV
Flowers peach-coloured, spotted, with recurved segments. Stems about 2.4 m (8 ft) tall. Mid summer. A clone selected from the Bullwood Hybrids.

'Peggy North' I(c)
Slightly scented orange flowers. The segments are strongly recurved and have brown spots, especially along the margin and in the centre. Height 1.2–1.5 m (4–5 ft). Mid summer.

'Phoebus' I(a)
Flowers yellow, upward-facing. Stems 1–

1.2 m (3–4 ft), with a few bulbils in the leaf axils. Mid summer. Good for forcing.

'Pink Beauty' VII(c)
Flat, rose-pink flowers with dark spots, the segments with paler margins. Height 1.5–2 m (5–6 ft). Late summer. The flowers can be as much as 25 cm (10 in) across.

'Pink Giant' I(c)
Pendent flowers, red, veined with carmine-pink inside and with an orange centre spotted with dark brown. Each segment is pale salmon on the back with a green-yellow central stripe. Height about 1 m (3 ft). Mid summer.

Pink Pearl Trumpets VI(a)
Scented, trumpet-shaped flowers, light pink inside, outside deep rose-pink or reddish purple. Height 1.2–1.5 m (4–5 ft). Mid to late summer. A grex selected from the Aurelian Hybrids.

Pink Perfection Strain VI(a)
Flowers scented, trumpet-shaped and drooping, purplish pink with bright orange anthers. Height 1.5–2 m (5–6 ft). Mid summer. Vigorous lilies that carry 15 to 20 flowers on a stem, and will grow well in partial shade. This grex was selected from a seedling whose parents were *L. leucanthum* and *L. sargentiae*.

'Pirate' I(a)
Flowers upward-facing, star-shaped, orange-red. Height about 1.2 m (4 ft). Early summer.

'Prosperity' I(b)
Flowers outward-facing, the lemon yellow segments recurved at the tips. The anthers are red. Height 80–120 cm (2½–4 ft). Mid summer. *L. amabile* var. *luteum* was one of the parents.

'Prune' I(a)
About six upward-facing flowers per stem, deep pink with brown spots. Each segment has a yellow margin. The pollen is reddish brown. Height 1–1.2 m (3–4 ft). Early to mid summer.

Red Band Hybrids VII(b)
Flowers scented, crimson-red to vermilion, each segment spotted with red, crinkly along the margin and often with a white border, recurved at the tip. Height 1.3–1.5 m (4½–5 ft). Late summer. These hybrids are derived from *L. auratum*.

'Red Night' see **'Roter Cardinal'**

'Redruth' I(b)
Outward-facing, rich red flowers. Height 1–1.2 m (3–4 ft). Early to mid summer. This lily is a cross between a red form of *L. lancifolium* and 'Enchantment'.

'Redstart' I(b)
Flowers outward-facing, mahogany red with heavy spotting and segments partly reflexed. Height 1–1.2 m (3–4 ft). Mid to late summer.

'Rosefire' I(a)
Flowers 6 to 20 per stem, red-orange, cup-shaped, upward-facing, each segment with a yellow blotch in the centre and a few spots towards the base. Stems about 1 m (3 ft). Early summer.

'Rosewood' IV
Pink flowers with a paler, spotted centre. Segments long and slender, widely spreading and reflexed. Height 2–2.2 m (6–7 ft). Mid summer. Selected from the Bullwood Hybrids, this tall lily is ideal for the back of a border or among shrubs.

'Rosita' I(a)
Flowers upward-facing, cup-shaped, greyish purple-pink with blackish spots in the centre. Anthers red-brown. Height 60–100 cm (2–3 ft). Early summer. The flowers are an unusual colour, rarely seen in lilies. 'Rosita' was produced when Asiatic Hybrids were crossed with *L. cernuum*.

'Roter Cardinal' I(a)
Cup-shaped, upward-facing flowers, deep maroon-red, spotted with black-purple in the throat. Height 75–100 cm (2½–3 ft). Early to mid summer. Sometimes found in catalogues under the name 'Red Night'.

'Roter Cardinal'
(see page 109)

'Safari' I(a)

Upward-facing flowers, orange, red in the centre, each segment with a yellow streak at the base and spotted with black. Stem about 1.2 m (4 ft) tall, reddish brown and carrying about 20 flowers. Mid summer.

'Sahara' I(a)

Flowers upward-facing, yellow-orange with darker veining, the throat slightly spotted with brown. The anthers are red-brown. Height about 60 cm (2 ft). Mid summer.

'Saint Blazey' I(b)

Flowers outward-facing, red, shading to orange-red at the centre. Height about 70 cm (2 ft 4 in). Mid summer.

'Saint Day' I(b)

Flowers outward-facing, red, changing to orange-red at the centre. Stem about 75 cm (2½ ft) tall, carrying 20 to 25 flowers. Mid summer. A clone selected from the Cornish Hybrids.

'Shuksan'

'Saint Just' I(a)

Flowers cup-shaped, about 12 per stem, red in the centre, shading to orange at the tips of the segments. Height about 60 cm (2 ft). Mid summer.

'Samba' I(a)

Upward-facing, deep yellow flowers with small brown spots in the centre and red-brown pollen. Height about 70 cm (2 ft 4 in). Early summer. A selection from the Sundrop grex.

San Gabriel Strain IV

Nodding, scented, turk's-cap flowers in various shades of yellow, spotted with black in the throat. Height 1.5–2 m (5–6 ft). Mid summer. There are usually 20 or more flowers per stem. A complex grex that includes *L. parryi* and *L. humboldtii* in its parentage.

'Sans Souci' VII(d)

White flowers suffused and spotted with red, the edges and tips of the segments white. Height about 1 m (3 ft). Mid to late summer. *L. speciosum* var. *rubrum* is included among the parents of this lily.

Sentinel Strain VI(a)

Up to 20 flowers to a stem, trumpet-shaped opening to bowl-shaped, white

with a yellow throat, each segment with a yellow-green stripe on the back. The pollen is dark brown. Height 1.2–1.5 m (4–5 ft). Early to mid summer. This grex was selected from *L. leucanthum* var. *centifolium*.

'Shuksan' IV
A hybrid between *L. humboldtii* and *L. pardalinum*. Up to 18 turk's-cap flowers per stem, yellow-orange, with sparse black or red-brown spots and the tips of the segments flushed with red. The pollen is orange. Height 1.2–2 m (4–6 ft). Mid summer. A selection from the Bellingham Hybrids – vigorous, hardy and easy to grow, and able to grow in semi-shady conditions.

'Simoen' I(a)
Flowers cup-shaped, upward-facing, pale orange-yellow with a pale yellow throat. Pollen orange-brown. Height 60–100 cm (2–3 ft). Early to mid summer. Often misspelt 'Simeon' in catalogues.

'Sinai' I(a)
Flowers upward-facing, pale orange, each segment edged with yellow. The anthers are brown. Height about 70 cm (2 ft 4 in). Early to mid summer.

'Sirocco' I(a)
Flowers cup-shaped, upward-facing, pale yellowish pink, darker in the throat and with brown spots. Pollen brown. Height 1–1.2 m (3–4 ft). Early to mid summer.

'Sonata' I(c)
Pendent turk's-cap flowers, pale coral-pink, pale orange in the centre, the segments with darker margins and dark spots. Height 1–1.2 m (3–4 ft). Mid summer. A hybrid between *L. cernuum* and *L. lancifolium*.

'Yellow Star' (see page 113)

'Sorrento' I(a)
Cup-shaped, carmine pink flowers with orange-buff blotches and a few dots in the centre. Each segment has a red margin. Height about 90 cm (3 ft). Mid summer. The stems carry about seven flowers.

'Star Gazer' VII(c)
Upward-facing, flat, red flowers with dark spots, the segments reflexed at the tips. Height about 1.5 m (5 ft). Mid summer. A good lily for forcing and for growing in pots. 'Journey's End' is often sold under this name – true 'Star Gazer' does not have the segments margined with white.

'Stardrift' VII(d)
Flowers purplish red, the segments with whitish margins and deep red spots. Pollen dark brown. Stems about 1.5 m (5 ft). Mid summer.

'Sterling Star' I(a)
Flowers cup-shaped, upward-facing, white, shaded with cream and speckled with brown dots. Height 1–1.2 m (3–4 ft). Early to mid summer. A pretty, sturdy lily, vigorous and reliable.

'Striped Beauty' I(a)
Cup-shaped, salmon-orange flowers, the throat pale yellow with a few brown spots. Each segment has a purple stripe. Height about 90 cm (3 ft). Early to mid summer. The stems usually carry about 15 flowers.

Sundrop I(a)
Flowers upward-facing, cup-shaped, golden yellow. Height 80–100 cm (2½–3 ft). Early summer.

'Sun Ray' I(a)
Upward-facing flowers, yellow with sparse brown spots and dark brown anthers. Height 1 m (3 ft). Early to mid summer.

'Sunny Twinkle' I(b)
Outward-facing, orange flowers with dark brown spots and rust-brown anthers. Height 90–100 cm (3 ft). Early to mid summer.

Sutter's Gold Strain I(c)
Nodding turk's-cap flowers, deep yellow, with the thick, waxy segments often dotted with red. Height 1–1.2 m (3–4 ft). Mid summer. Easily grown, long-lasting lilies that are quick to increase. A complex grex with *L. cernuum* and *L. lancifolium* in the parentage.

'Sylvester' I(a)
Flowers cup-shaped, golden yellow, 6 to 8 per stem. Height about 60 cm (2 ft). Early summer. A selection from the Sundrop grex.

'Theseus' I(c)
Scented flowers, rich red, pendent and with recurved segments. Height 1.5–2 m (5–6 ft). Mid summer.

'Tiger White' I(c)
Flowers nodding, white with a greenish throat, the recurved segments with a few maroon-purple spots. The pollen is brown-orange. Stem 1–1.2 m (3–4 ft), carrying 10 to 20 flowers. Mid to late summer. A hybrid whose parents include *L. lancifolium* and *L. amabile*. It is sometimes erroneously listed in catalogues as 'White Tiger'.

'Trance' VII(b)
Scented flowers, soft pink with pale spots in the centre, each segment darker in the centre and almost white at the edge. Height 60–100 cm (2–3 ft). Early to mid summer.

'Troubadour' VII(c)
Flat, scented, white to pink flowers, each segment with crinkly edges, a recurved tip, a central crimson-red stripe and crimson-red spots. The anthers are red. Height about 1 m (3 ft). Late summer to early autumn.

'Truro' I(c)
Flowers orange-red, spotted. Height about 90 cm (3 ft). Early to mid summer.

'Tsingense' II
Brilliant orange flowers with tiny black

spots in the centre. Height 1.5–2 m (5–6 ft). Mid summer. A cross, made in 1977, between *L.* × *dalhansonii* and *L. tsingtauense*.

'Utopia' I(a)

Flowers cup-shaped, buttercup yellow with a greenish throat and a few black spots near the centre. The segments are slightly recurved at the tips. Light brown pollen. Height about 1.4 m (4½ ft). Early to mid summer. The stems bear 8 to 20 flowers.

'Venture' I(a)

Upward-facing, bright red flowers with black spots and the segments slightly recurved at the tips. Height 1.5 m (5 ft). Early to mid summer. The stems bear 8 to 25 flowers and are slightly downy.

'Viking' I(c)

Flowers nodding, the segments reflexed, orange-red. Height 1.2–1.5 m (4–5 ft). Mid summer. Produced when *L. davidii* var. *willmottiae* was crossed with *L. lancifolium*.

'White Happiness' I(a)

Flowers cup-shaped, upward-facing, ivory white with dark red spots towards the centre and brown anthers. Height 45–60 cm (1½–2 ft). Early summer.

'White Lady' VI(a)

Trumpet-shaped flowers, white with a yellow-green throat and pale brownish stripes outside. The pollen is orange. Height about 1.5 m (5 ft). Mid summer.

'White Mountain' VII(c)

Flowers flat, white with yellowish green in the throat, each segment spotted with greyish red and with a yellow midrib. Height about 1 m (3 ft). Mid summer.

'White Tiger' see **'Tiger White'**

'Yellow Blaze' I(a)

Flowers upward-facing, cup-shaped, yellow with spots. Height 1.2–1.5 m (4–5 ft). Mid to late summer.

'Yellow Ribbons' VII(c)

Flowers flat, white with a green throat, each segment with orange-yellow bands and a few golden spots. Pollen orange-brown. Height about 1.2 m (4 ft). Late summer.

'Yellow Star' I(b)

Flowers outward-facing, cup-shaped, yellow with small brown spots and brown pollen. Height 1–1.2 m (3–4 ft). Mid summer.

'Zephyr' I(a)

Upward-facing, cup-shaped, soft pink flowers with many small black spots, darker outside, and with dark brown pollen. Height 1.2–1.5 m (4–5 ft). Early summer. There can be as many as 25 flowers on each stem.

Lilies for Selected Sites

The following lists contain species and hybrids suitable for particular purposes and places. To some extent the choice is subjective, and as readers become familiar with growing lilies they will select their own favourites.

EASY LILIES FOR BEGINNERS

L. columbianum
L. dauricum
L. hansonii
L. henryi
L. lancifolium and its varieties
L. martagon
L. pyrenaicum
L. regale
Bellingham Hybrids
'Black Beauty'
'Black Dragon'
'Bright Star'
Citronella Strain
'Connecticut King'
'Enchantment'
'Eros'
Golden Clarion Strain
Harlequin Strain
Mid-Century Hybrids
Sutter's Gold Strain

LILIES FOR FULL SUN

L. amabile
L. canadense
L. candidum
L. formosanum
L. longiflorum
L. martagon var. *album*
L. pardalinum
L. pumilum
L. regale
Fiesta Hybrids
Harlequin Strain
Mid-Century Hybrids

LILIES FOR SEMI-SHADE OR WOODLAND

L. hansonii
L. lancifolium and its varieties
L. mackliniae
L. martagon
L. speciosum
L. superbum
L. wardii
African Queen Strain
Copper King Strain
Paisley Strain
Pink Perfection Strain
'Shuksan'
Cardiocrinum species

Opposite: *Lilium pumilum* is a short-growing lily with small flowers, making it a good choice for a rock garden or raised bed (see also page 89)

Lilies for herbaceous or mixed borders

L. auratum

L. chalcedonicum

L. candidum

L. davidii

L. henryi

L. lancifolium and its varieties

L. monadelphum

L. pardalinum

L. pumilum

L. pyrenaicum

L. regale

L. speciosum, its varieties and cultivars

Aurelian Hybrids

Harlequin Strain

'Limelight'

Mid-Century Hybrids

Moonlight Strain

Lilies for rock gardens and raised beds

L. amabile

L. cernuum

L. formosanum var. *pricei*

L. nanum

L. oxypetalum

L. pomponium

L. pumilum

L. rubellum

Tall lilies

L. auratum

L. henryi

L. humboldtii

L. lancifolium var. *splendens*

L. leichtlinii var. *maximowiczii*

L. leucanthum var. *centifolium*

L. pardalinum var. *giganteum*

L. superbum

Bellingham Hybrids

Bullwood Hybrids

'Lake Tulare'

'Viking'

Cardiocrinum giganteum

Lilies for containers

L. auratum

L. formosanum

L. lancifolium and its varieties

L. longiflorum

L. nepalense

L. pumilum

L. speciosum, its varieties and cultivars

'Black Dragon'

'Cambridge'

'Connecticut King'

'Dukat'

'Feuerzauber'

Fiesta Hybrids

'Green Dragon'

Jamboree Strain

'Star Gazer'

LILIES FOR LIMY SOILS

L. amabile
L. bulbiferum var. croceum
L. candidum
L. chalcedonicum
L. concolor
L. henryi
L. martagon

L. monadelphum
L. pomponium
L. pyrenaicum
L. × testaceum
'Bright Star'
Martagon hybrids

LILIES THAT DEMAND ACID SOILS

L. auratum
L. canadense
L. pardalinum
L. rubellum
L. sargentiae

L. speciosum, its varieties and cultivars
L. superbum
Bellingham Hybrids
Other American Hybrids (Div. IV)

ESPECIALLY FRAGRANT LILIES

L. auratum
L. candidum
L. cernuum
L. hansonii
L. regale

L. speciosum
L. × testaceum
Oriental Hybrids
Many trumpet lilies in Div. VI(a)

LILIES FOR CUTTING

L. auratum
L. formosanum
L. × hollandicum
L. lancifolium and its varieties
L. longiflorum
L. pardalinum
L. speciosum, its varieties and cultivars

'Corsage'
'Enchantment'
Fiesta Hybrids
Harlequin Strain
'King Pete'
Mid-Century Hybrids

Glossary

acid Soil with a pH of less than 7; such soil is often peaty.

alkaline Soil with a pH of more than 7; applies to chalky or limy soils.

anther The pollen-containing terminal part of a stamen.

basal plate The solid tissue at the bottom of a bulb, to which the bulb scales are attached.

bulb scale One of the fleshy 'leaves' that together form the bulb.

bulb-tunic The dead, papery, leathery or fibrous coat or covering that surrounds most bulbs.

bulbil A small bulb formed on the stem, often in the leaf axil.

bulblet A small underground bulb that develops from the parent bulb.

capsule A dry fruit that splits open when ripe to release the seeds.

ciliate Having the margin fringed with hairs.

claw The narrow, elongated basal part of a perianth segment.

clone Plants derived from the vegetative reproduction of an individual, and all possessing the same genetic constitution. The name of a clone is written within single quotation marks, e.g. 'Black Dragon'.

compost A mixture of ingredients used for potting or seed-sowing. Also describes rotted organic material.

cotyledon A seed leaf, i.e. a leaf formed inside the seed.

cultivar A variant of a species or hybrid, which is of horticultural worth or interest and is maintained in cultivation.

dorsifixed An anther that is attached to its stalk by its back, at about the mid-point.

epigeal Type of germination in which the cotyledon emerges above soil level.

filament The stalk of a stamen which bears the anther at the top.

form (written as forma or f.) Unit of classification below that of species, subspecies or variety. It is usually differentiated by only one characteristic.

genus A group of related species (rarely only one species) that have certain characteristics in common.

grex A range of hybrids, all derived from the same parents. The name, unlike that of a clone, is not enclosed in quotation marks when written, e.g. Bellingham Hybrids.

hypogeal Type of germination in which the cotyledon remains below soil level.

humus Well-rotted organic matter, e.g. leafmould, peat, animal manure.

hybrid The result of a cross between two plants belonging to different species, subspecies, varieties or forms.

inflorescence Grouping of flowers on the main flower stem.

leaf axil The upper angle between the leaf and the stem that bears it.

Opposite: 'Pirate' is a lily of medium height, here growing in a mixed border with blue *Iris latifolia* (see page 109)

leafmould Humus produced from rotted leaves.

mulch A layer of loose material such as bracken, compost or chipped bark, laid on top of the soil as frost protection or extra nutrition.

nectary furrow Groove at the base of a perianth segment in which the nectary (which produces nectar) lies.

ovary Ovule-containing part of the flower, situated at the base of the style. When mature it becomes the fruit capsule.

ovule Structure from which the seed develops after pollination.

papilla A small, blunt, wart-like protuberance.

pedicel A stalk that usually carries one flower.

perianth segment One of the parts of the perianth (the collective term for the similar-looking sepals and petals).

raceme An elongated arrangement of flowers, similar to a flower-spike but in which each flower is stalked; in a compound raceme there are two or more flowers on each primary stalk.

rhizome A modified, usually underground stem that can produce roots and shoots.

rosette A cluster of leaves arising at the base of a stem and radiating in all directions.

scattered Leaves that are distributed up and around the stem.

seed coat The hard outer covering of a seed.

species A unit of classification below that of genus.

stamen The male part of a flower, consisting of a filament (stalk) and anther, which contains the pollen.

stem root A root produced on the stem.

stigma The expanded tip of the style to which pollen sticks when the flower is pollinated – in lilies the stigma is usually three-lobed.

stolon Slender underground growth produced by a bulb, which produces a small bulb at its tip.

strain see **grex**

style The usually slender structure above the ovary, which bears the stigma at its tip.

subspecies (written as subsp.) The unit of classification below that of species.

umbel Arrangement of flowers in which all the flower stalks arise from the top of the main stem.

variety (written as var.) Unit of classification below that of species or subspecies.

vegetative propagation Method of increasing plants other than by seed, e.g. by taking cuttings, division, scales, bulblets.

whorled Leaves that are borne like wheel-spokes, at intervals up the stem.

Bibliography

Fox, D. *Growing Lilies* Croom Helm, 1985.

Matthews, V.A. '*Lilium*' in Walters, S. et al. *European Garden Flora* 1: 193–206
  Cambridge University Press, 1986.

Rockwell, F.F., Grayson, E.C. and de Graaff, J. *The Complete Book of Lilies* Doubleday & Co.
  Inc., 1961.

Synge, P.M. *Lilies* Batsford, 1980.

Woodcock, H.B.D. and Stearn, W.T. *Lilies of the World* Country Life 1950.

Curtis's Botanical Magazine (now *The Kew Magazine*). This publication still maintains its long
  tradition of fine colour printing and articles on plants, plant collecting and conservation.
  Since it was established in 1787 nearly 10,500 colour plates have appeared by many of the
  best British botanical artists.

The following publications are produced by the Lily Societies in Britain and North America:

The Lily Year Book Volumes 1–34 (Royal Horticultural Society, 1932–70). Renamed *Lilies and
  Allied Plants* (1971). Renamed *Lilies and other Liliaceae* (1972–79). Issued as *RHS Lily Group
  Bulletin* (1981–82). Now entitled *Lilies and related Plants* (published annually from 1984).

Yearbook of the North American Lily Society (North American Lily Society, published annually
  from 1948).

SOCIETIES

The Royal Horticultural Society Lily Group

Hon. Membership Secretary: Dr A.F. Hayward, Rosemary Cottage, Lowbands, Redmarley,
  Gloucestershire GL9 3NG, England

The North American Lily Society, Inc.

Executive Secretary: Mrs Dorothy B. Schaefer, P.O. Box 476, Waukee, Iowa 50263, USA

Acknowledgements

Line Artwork by Ron Hayward.

Photographs

Brinsley Burbidge, pages 15, 31, 82 (top); Linda Burgess/Insight, page 67; Crown
copyright © reproduced with the permission of the Controller, Her Majesty's Stationery
Office, and the Director, Royal Botanic Gardens, Kew, pages 6, 10, 12, 18; Christopher Grey-
Wilson, page 83 (bottom); Hamlyn Publishing Group Limited/W.F. Davidson, pages 34, 58;
Jerry Harpur, pages 14, 94 (top); Andrew Lawson, pages 22, 27, 30, 35, 38, 42, 46, 50, 55, 62,
63, 70–1, 74, 75, 79 (top and bottom), 82 (bottom), 83 (top), 86 (top), 90, 91 (bottom), 98
(bottom), 103, 107 (top and bottom), 114; Brian Mathew, pages 66, 78 (top), 86 (bottom), 87
(top), 91 (top), 95, 98 (top), 99, 110 (top), 111, 118; S & O Mathews, page 102 (top); Victoria
Matthews, pages 23, 78 (bottom), 87 (bottom), 98 (bottom), 102 (bottom), 106; Photos
Horticultural, pages 39, 110 (bottom); David Rae, page 59.

Index